sam shepard

——————— ■ ———————

states of shock
far north
silent tongue

Sam Shepard has written more than forty plays, eleven of which have won Obie awards. In 1979 he was awarded the Pulitzer Prize for Drama for *Buried Child,* and in 1984 he gained an Oscar nomination as best supporting actor for his performance in *The Right Stuff. A Lie of the Mind* was named the Best New Play of the 1985–86 season by the New York Drama Critics Circle.

Earlier in his career, Mr. Shepard spent several seasons with off-off-Broadway groups such as La Mama and Café Cino, and was for several years playwright in residence at the Magic Theater in San Francisco. He has also performed in the movies *Days of Heaven, Resurrection, Raggedy Man, Frances, Country, Fool for Love* (adapted from his own play), *Crimes of the Heart, Steel Magnolias, Voyager, Defenseless, Bright Angel,* and *Thunderheart.*

In 1988 Shepard wrote and directed *Far North,* starring Jessica Lange, Tess Harper, and Charles Durning. Previous credits as a screenwriter include *Zabriskie Point* and *Paris, Texas,* which won the Palme d'Or at the 1984 Cannes Film Festival.

In the spring of 1986 he was elected to the American Academy of Arts and Letters.

states of shock

far north

silent tongue

sam shepard

vintage books

A DIVISION OF RANDOM HOUSE, INC.

NEW YORK

Library of Congress Cataloging-in-Publication Data
Shepard, Sam, 1943–
[States of shock]
States of shock; Far north; Silent tongue / Sam Shepard.-
p.   cm.
ISBN 978-0-679-74218-0
1. Motion picture plays.   I. Shepard, Sam, 1943–   Far north.
1992.   II. Shepard, Sam, 1943–   Silent tongue. 1992.   III. Title:
States of shock.   IV. Title: Far north.   V. Title: Silent tongue.
PS3569.H394A6   1992
812'.54—dc20   92–50639
CIP

Grateful acknowledgment is made to the following for permission to reprint previously published material: *Ludlow Music, Inc.:* "Goodnight Irene" words and music by Huddie Ledbetter and John A. Lomax. TRO—© Copyright 1936 (renewed) 1950 (renewed) Ludlow Music, Inc., New York, New York. Used by permission. *Fisher Music Corporation* and *Lindabet Music:* Excerpt from "Good Morning Heartache" by Dan Fisher, Irene Higginbotham, and Ervin Drake. Reprinted by permission of Fisher Music Corporation and Lindabet Music, care of Songwriters Guild of America on behalf of Lindabet Music.

Manufactured in the United States of America

146689836

contents

states of shock

a vaudeville nightmare

"You might come here Sunday on a whim.
Say your life broke down. The last good kiss
you had was years ago. You walk these streets
laid out by the insane, past hotels
that didn't last, bars that did, the tortured try
of local drivers to accelerate their lives.
Only churches are kept up. The jail
turned 70 this year. The only prisoner
is always in, not knowing what he's done.

The principal supporting business now
is rage."

Richard Hugo

States of Shock was first presented by The American Place Theatre (Wynn Handman, Artistic Director) in New York City on April 30, 1991. It was directed by Bill Hart; the set design was by Bill Stabile; the costume design was by Gabriel Berry; the lighting design was by Pat Dignan and Anne Militello; the sound design was by J. A. Deane; and the production stage manager was Lloyd Davis, Jr. The cast was as follows:

COLONEL	John Malkovich
STUBBS	Michael Wincott
GLORY BEE	Erica Gimpel
WHITE MAN	Steve Nelson
WHITE WOMAN	Isa Thomas

Bare stage. Cyclorama upstage covering entire wall and into ceiling. Simple café table and two chairs upstage right. Red Naugahyde café booth with table downstage left. Seated in the two chairs, upstage right, facing each other, are the WHITE WOMAN and the WHITE MAN. The WHITE MAN sits slumped in his chair with his chin on his chest and his hands folded in his lap, facing stage right. He is not asleep but appears to be in a deep state of catharsis. Very still. The WHITE WOMAN, sitting opposite him at the table, is more upright but equally still, staring off into upstage space. Her hands are folded on the purse in her lap. They are both dressed completely in white, very expensive outfits, reminiscent of West Palm Beach. She has a wide-brimmed straw hat and elaborate jeweled dark glasses. Their faces and hands are also white and pallid, like cadavers.

In the darkness, the sounds of two live percussionists situated behind the cyclorama, extreme right and left, opposite each other. Their driving rhythms slowly build in intensity as the cyclorama takes on an ominous tone. The cyclorama is lit up with tracer fire, rockets, explosions in the night. A cross-fade takes place in which the war panorama and drumming are exchanged for the stage light and the silence of the white couple who just sit there very still but not with the sense that they're frozen in time. A pause.

A referee's whistle is sharply blown off stage left. From stage left enters the COLONEL, dressed in a strange ensemble of military uniforms and paraphernalia that have no apparent rhyme or reason: an air force captain's khaki hat from WW II, a marine sergeant's coat with various medals and pins dangling from the chest and shoulders, knickers with leather leggings below the knees, and a Civil War saber hanging from his waist. The COLONEL is pushing

STUBBS *in a wheelchair with small American flags, raccoon tails, and various talismans and good-luck charms flapping and dangling from the back of the seat and armrests.* STUBBS *is dressed in a long-sleeved black shirt and black jeans. He's covered from the waist to the ankles with an old army blanket. A silver whistle hangs around his neck by a red string.*

They come to a stop downstage center. STUBBS *stares straight ahead and blows his whistle again. The white couple turn their heads toward* STUBBS *and the* COLONEL, *acknowledging their presence, then return to their previous attitudes and postures—very still. Another pause.*

COLONEL: I believe this might be the deal right here, Stubbs. Might be just the ticket. *(*GLORY BEE, *a waitress in uniform, pencil stuck in her hair, carrying menus and a serving tray, enters from right.)*

GLORY BEE: Yessir. Two for lunch? Do you have a smoking preference?

COLONEL: I prefer smoking, don't you? Country was founded on tobacco. Don't see any reason not to support it.

GLORY BEE: That's fine, sir. Would you follow me, please. *(She moves toward booth, left.)*

COLONEL: What we'd like is something with a view. My friend here just got out of the hospital and he's been yearning to gaze into an open vista for some time now.

GLORY BEE: Would a booth be all right, sir? You can see the window from here. Best view in the house. *(She stops by the red booth and motions toward upstage.)*

COLONEL: How's that suit you, Stubbs? The booth? *(*STUBBS *just stares upstage at the cyclorama. Pause. To* GLORY BEE.) He's suffered a uh—kind of disruption. Temporary kind of thing, they say. Takes some time to unscramble.

GLORY BEE: I see.

COLONEL: Shot smack through the chest is what it was. Show the lady, Stubbs. (STUBBS *blows his whistle again and abruptly lifts his shirt to the armpits, revealing a massive red scar in the center of his chest.* GLORY BEE *looks away from it.* STUBBS *keeps his shirt held up.*) Took a direct hit from a ninety millimeter. Went straight through him. Killed my son who, unfortunately, was standing right behind him. Killed him dead. Stubbs is the lucky one. It's a wonder he's still with us. Isn't that right, Stubbs? (STUBBS *just stares with his shirt still up. To* GLORY BEE.) 'Course my son never knew what hit him. Thank the good Lord. But today, you see—today—what is your name, miss?

GLORY BEE: Uh—Glory.

COLONEL: Glory. Isn't that fine. "Glory."

GLORY BEE: "Glory Bee."

COLONEL: How 'bout that. "Glory Bee." Has a kind of a French ring to it. Well—anyhow, today happens to be the anniversary of my son's death. So, what I thought was I'd just pick up Stubbs here from the hospital and take him out for a dessert of some kind. Maybe a hot fudge sundae or something on that order.

GLORY BEE: That's fine. Um—is the booth—okay?

COLONEL: Booth's fine. Booth's gonna be just perfect. You can pull your shirt down now, Stubbs. We're gonna park it right here. (STUBBS *pulls his shirt down as* COLONEL *wheels him around to the upstage right side of the table.* GLORY BEE *lays the menus out on the table.*)

GLORY BEE: Would you like some coffee or a beverage of some kind, sir?

COLONEL: Coffee? Coffee, Stubbs? (STUBBS *nods. To* GLORY BEE.) You wouldn't happen to have any "Maker's Mark," would you? Kentucky bourbon? "Fighting Cock"? Something with a little sting to it?

GLORY BEE: No, sir. This is a family restaurant.

COLONEL: Families don't drink bourbon?

GLORY BEE: Well, we don't have a liquor license, sir. This is a coffee shop.

COLONEL: I see. Well, make it two coffees, then. That'd be just dandy. A "cuppa' joe."

GLORY BEE: Thank you, sir. I'll be back in just a minute. *(GLORY BEE exits right. COLONEL spits in his hand and smooths STUBBS's hair carefully.)*

COLONEL *(as he tends to STUBBS)*: This is a family restaurant, Stubbs. How 'bout that. Guess we got lucky. Could've wound up any old place. Wandered into a titty bar or roadhouse dive, but here we are in a family restaurant. God knows we've had worse luck on a Sunday. *(COLONEL settles into booth, handing one of the menus to STUBBS who just stares at it. COLONEL looks through the menu. The white couple turn their heads and stare at STUBBS and the COLONEL. Looking through menu.)* Let's just see what they've got here in the way of desserts. That's what you want now? You've made your mind up on that? No main course for you? *(STUBBS nods.)* Okee-dokee. *(COLONEL removes his hat and rubs his bald head.)* Grass don't grow on a busy street. Well, then, let's see— They've got a peach cobbler. That might be nice. Some kinda sauce on it. They got a key lime pie. Isn't that somethin'. Didn't think we were that far south for key lime pie. How's that sound to you, Stubbs? Key lime? *(STUBBS just stares at him. Pause.)* It's a pale green kind of a thing. *(No response from STUBBS.)*

WHITE WOMAN *(to COLONEL, out of the blue)*: We've been waiting three quarters of an hour. Can you imagine that? *(COLONEL turns to her.)*

COLONEL: Excuse me?

WHITE WOMAN: My husband and I have been waiting three quarters of an hour for a simple order.

WHITE MAN: Clam chowder.

WHITE WOMAN: That's right. Two bowls of clam chowder. You'd think that would be simple enough.

COLONEL: You'd think so, wouldn't you.

WHITE WOMAN: I mean it's not as though we ordered a club sandwich or a turkey dinner with a lot of trimmings. *(Pause. COLONEL turns back to STUBBS and the menu. STUBBS suddenly blows his whistle and talks directly to the white couple, who just stare at him.)*

STUBBS *(to white couple)*: When I was hit— It went straight through me. Out the other side. Someone was killed. But it wasn't me. I'm not the one. I'm the lucky one. *(Pause. The white couple just stare at STUBBS for a moment, then turn back to their previous attitudes. STUBBS keeps staring at them as though waiting for a response. COLONEL refers to the menu.)*

COLONEL *(still studying menu)*: They've got your standard banana split. How 'bout that, Stubbs? No frills.

STUBBS *(to white couple)*: When I was hit—I never saw it coming. I never heard a sound. The sky went white. *(GLORY BEE enters from right, very slowly, balancing two cups of coffee on her tray which she is having great difficulty with. Coffee keeps sloshing over the edge of the cups as she stares intensely at them and moves inch by inch toward the COLONEL and STUBBS in the booth. The white couple stare at GLORY BEE as she makes her way. COLONEL keeps focused on the menu.)*

WHITE WOMAN: There she is.

WHITE MAN: She ought to be fired.

WHITE WOMAN: Oh, miss! Miss! *(GLORY BEE ignores them and keeps heading toward the booth with the coffee. All her attention on the cups.)*

GLORY BEE *(to herself, about spilling coffee)*: Dang it! Dang, dang, dang, dang, dang!

WHITE MAN: She's ignoring us.

WHITE WOMAN: MISS! *(*GLORY BEE *keeps heading painstakingly toward the booth, trying to balance the coffee.)*

COLONEL *(to* STUBBS*)*: What about a pair of banana splits? Or would you rather have the hot fudge? It's up to you, Stubbs.

STUBBS *(to white couple)*: When I was hit— The lights went out. It's been dark ever since.

WHITE WOMAN *(to* GLORY BEE*)*: We have better things to do this morning than wait three quarters of an hour for two bowls of clam chowder.

GLORY BEE *(to* COLONEL*, as she reaches booth)*: Excuse me, sir, but would you mind taking these for me. I have the darnedest time balancing liquids. I don't know what it is. Ever since I was very little.

COLONEL *(as he takes coffee off tray)*: That's because you stare at the cups.

GLORY BEE: Excuse me?

COLONEL: You can't stare at the cups. You've got to fix your attention on a point in space. You've got to ignore the cups altogether.

GLORY BEE: I see.

COLONEL *(placing cups on table)*: You've got to pretend the cups don't exist. There's a trick to it.

WHITE MAN: She's completely ignoring us.

COLONEL: Otherwise you're bound to spill.

GLORY BEE: I'll have to try that. *(*STUBBS *suddenly lifts his shirt again and shows his scar to* GLORY BEE.*)*

STUBBS (*to* GLORY BEE): Right here is where it went through. It went clear through here and out the other side.

COLONEL: Stubbs, put your shirt down now. The lady's already seen that. (STUBBS *pulls his shirt back down and stares at the* COLONEL, *who continues perusing the menu.*)

GLORY BEE (*to* COLONEL): Have you decided on something, sir?

COLONEL: Well, let's see—

WHITE WOMAN: We could have had most of our shopping done by now. We could be buying things as we speak.

COLONEL: I think what we're gonna do is have us a pair of banana splits. That okay by you, Stubbs? (STUBBS *just stares at him.*)

GLORY BEE (*writing down order*): Two banana splits.

COLONEL: Yeah. I think that's right. And would you mind putting a little candle right in the center of each one of those. You've got those little birthday candles, don't ya?

GLORY BEE: Birthday candle.

COLONEL: Yeah. You know, those little pink and blue jobs like you have for the kids? Just to honor my son. Just as a kind of reminder.

GLORY BEE: You want two birthday candles?

COLONEL: One each. Right smack in the center. Just as a token.

GLORY BEE: You don't want me to sing or anything, do you? I'm capable of singing, but I don't like doing it at the drop of a hat.

COLONEL: Sing? No. No singing. This isn't his birthday.

GLORY BEE: Who?

COLONEL: My son. It's the anniversary of his death. Not his birthday.

GLORY BEE: Oh. I thought *this* was your son.

COLONEL: No, no. This is the man who attempted to save my son's life by placing his body in the way of incoming artillery fire. I already told you that.

GLORY BEE: I'm sorry. We've been very busy. I *can* sing though, if you want me to.

COLONEL: No singing. That won't be necessary.

STUBBS *(to GLORY BEE)*: When I was hit I could no longer get my "thing" up. It just hangs there now. Like dead meat. Like road kill. *(Short pause. GLORY BEE stares at STUBBS, then pulls away.)*

GLORY BEE: Two banana splits. With candles.

COLONEL: Don't forget those candles, now.

GLORY BEE: No, sir. *(She crosses back, right. The white couple stop her.)*

WHITE WOMAN: Miss!

GLORY BEE: Yes, ma'am?

WHITE WOMAN: What in the name of Christ has happened to our clam chowder? We've been waiting three quarters of an hour.

GLORY BEE: I offered you the "Express" and you turned it down.

WHITE MAN: We could be shopping as we speak. *(STUBBS blows his whistle, then suddenly screams at GLORY BEE.)*

STUBBS: MY THING HANGS LIKE DEAD MEAT!!! *(Pause. White couple turns and stares at STUBBS. The COLONEL ignores them. He's busy taking several toy soldiers, tanks, airplanes, and ships out of his bag and arranging them on the table in front of him. STUBBS just stares into space.)*

WHITE WOMAN *(to GLORY BEE)*: I thought this was supposed to be a family restaurant.

GLORY BEE: It is. *(GLORY BEE exits right. Pause.)*

COLONEL *(moving toys around on table)*: She thought *you* were my son. Now. When you were hit, Stubbs—you were backed up against the mountain. Is that right? Pretend the sugar is the mountain. Right here. Just pretend. *(COLONEL moves the sugar dispenser into position.)*

STUBBS: Backed up against the mountain.

COLONEL: You had heavy enemy artillery plus warships firing into you from offshore. Let's say the knives will represent the shoreline. *(COLONEL moves knives into position. STUBBS picks up a fork.)*

STUBBS: Fork.

COLONEL: Forks? All right—fine—forks. That's fine. We'll say the forks are the shoreline. Forks will do well enough. *(COLONEL exchanges the knives for the forks and marks the hypothetical shoreline.)* Now—from the top of the mountain— Let me get this straight, now. Only you can verify this because you were there, Stubbs. I'm just going on hearsay. From the top of the mountain you were backed up by your own defensive artillery plus militia. Is that right? *(STUBBS just stares at the forks and toys.)* Does that seem right to you? The way I've got it set up? You're the expert on this. *(STUBBS reaches over from his wheelchair and moves one of the toy pieces into a different position.)* Good. Is that pretty close to the way it was? *(STUBBS just stares at the table.)* So, in effect, you were caught in a cross fire? Isn't that fair to say? You were backed up against the mountain, being fired upon by enemy artillery while your own defense continued to pound them from behind you. Firing across your heads. There was nowhere to run.

STUBBS: When I was hit—

COLONEL: Now hold your horses. Just wait a second. We'll get to that. I want to reconstruct everything up to that moment.

I know we've done this before, but there's certain particulars that still escape me.

STUBBS: When I was hit there was no sound.

COLONEL: I realize that! You're jumping the gun. That's not important now. What I'm trying to figure out is the exact configuration. The positions of each element. A catastrophe has to be examined from every possible angle. It has to be studied coldly, from the outside, without investing a lot of stupid emotion.

STUBBS: I was hit in silence.

COLONEL (*slamming table with his fist*): THAT MAKES NO DIF-FERENCE!! (*An explosion offstage in the distance. Pause. Silence. They stare at each other. The white couple is staring at them. Suddenly* STUBBS *backs his wheelchair up and then wheels himself over to the white couple. He parks the wheelchair upstage of their table. Still in booth.*) Stubbs! Don't be childish. We have to face this thing together. You know that as well as I do. There's no point in running off in a huff. Sooner or later we have to face it.

STUBBS (*to white couple*): The middle of me is all dead. The core. I'm eighty percent mutilated. The part of me that goes on living has no memory of the parts that are all dead. They've been separated for all time. They'll never have a partner. You're lucky to have a partner.

COLONEL: Stubbs! Front and center! Scat like a scalded dog! (STUBBS *wheels himself away from the white couple and returns to the booth where the* COLONEL *is pouring some whiskey from a silver flask into the two cups of* GLORY BEE*'s coffee.* STUBBS *parks by the booth and the* COLONEL.) Now, look, Stubbs—let's have an understanding here—all right? We're in a public situation. We have to use a little diplomacy. Some discretion. Restraint. You have to remember that the enemy is always sneaking. Always slimy. Lurking. Ready to snatch the slightest secret. The smallest slipup. Here— Have a drink. I've doctored it up some. Go ahead. It'll open your pipes. (COLONEL *offers a cup of coffee laced with whiskey out to* STUBBS. STUBBS *takes it but hesitates to drink. Pause.*) Well, go ahead. It's perfectly good whiskey. I've never steered you wrong on that score, have I? After all, you're not exactly a candidate for assassination, are you? Let's not get carried away with ourselves. (STUBBS *drinks.*) That's the ticket! No point in getting worked up over nothing. We're in this together. Let's have a toast. (*They click cups and drink together.*) TO THE ENEMY!

STUBBS (*holding his cup high*): TO THE ENEMY!

COLONEL: Exactly. WITHOUT THE ENEMY WE'RE NOTHING!

STUBBS (*toasting*): WITHOUT THE ENEMY WE'RE NOTHING!

COLONEL: Exactly. Where would we be today without the enemy?

STUBBS: I don't know . . . where would we be?

COLONEL: THE ENEMY HAS BROUGHT US TOGETHER!

STUBBS: THE ENEMY HAS BROUGHT US TOGETHER!

COLONEL: Exactly right. Now, there's no point in pouring your heart out to strangers, Stubbs. You oughta know that by now. No future in it. Where has it ever gotten you? Nowhere. Plain and simple. Absolutely nowhere. We have to stick together in this. We've got a history. Nobody knows that better than you and me. Best a stranger can do is pretend and we're both past that, aren't we, Stubbs?

STUBBS (*toasting*): WE'RE BOTH PAST THAT!

COLONEL: That's the truth of it. Pretending is not for us. What we're after is the hard facts. The bare bones.

STUBBS *(toasting)*: THE BARE BONES!

COLONEL: Exactly.

WHITE WOMAN: Would you both pipe down over there. This is a family restaurant.

WHITE MAN: That's absolutely right. *(COLONEL turns and stares at WHITE WOMAN and takes another drink, then turns back to the toys and speaks to STUBBS in a hushed, conspiratorial tone. WHITE WOMAN leans out of her chair toward the COLONEL, trying to eavesdrop.)*

COLONEL *(hushed)*: Now look, Stubbs— The placement of these two figures right here is the key to the whole thing. You see these two? *(COLONEL holds up two toy infantrymen and shows them to STUBBS.)* The red one is you and the white one is my son. Have you got that? Here— Take a look at them. Check them over carefully and memorize the colors. Try to study every detail. Every nuance. Let nothing escape your scrutiny. *(STUBBS takes the two toys and turns them over in his hands, examining them closely. Pause.)* Red and white. Red is you. White's my son. Okay? Have you got that? Are we on the same wavelength? *(STUBBS just stares.)* Now, what I'm gonna ask you to do is place those figures down in exactly the right positions for me. Only you can know this, Stubbs. Place them exactly where you and my son were standing when the artillery struck you.

STUBBS *(holding toy soldiers)*: Red and white.

COLONEL: That's correct.

STUBBS: And blue.

COLONEL: No! No blue. Just red and white.

STUBBS: And blue.

COLONEL: NO BLUE, STUBBS! NO BLUE!

WHITE WOMAN: We're trying to have a peaceful time here, if you don't mind. *(COLONEL crosses to WHITE WOMAN, whispers in her ear, then returns to the booth.)*

COLONEL *(to STUBBS)*: Place them down in the battlefield exactly as you were positioned on that fateful day. Now, just remember that the sugar is the mountain and the forks are the . . .

STUBBS: Shoreline.

COLONEL: Go ahead. *(GLORY BEE enters from right with the banana splits on her tray. She is carrying them much the same way as she was trying to balance the coffee—moving very slowly with all her attention on the tray. Candles are burning in the center of each banana split. The candles are much bigger than birthday candles.)*

WHITE MAN: There she is.

WHITE WOMAN: She ought to be shot.

WHITE MAN: Oh, miss! *(GLORY BEE keeps heading for the booth with the banana splits, ignoring the white couple.)*

WHITE WOMAN: She's ignoring us again.

WHITE MAN: Is that our order? That's not our order, is it?

WHITE WOMAN: No, it's not. It's *their* order.

WHITE MAN: We've been here longer than them, haven't we?

WHITE WOMAN: We've been here forever. *(GLORY BEE keeps steadfastly heading toward the booth, balancing the banana splits.)*

COLONEL: Set them down, Stubbs.

STUBBS *(holding toys)*: Blue is me?

COLONEL: *White* is you! There is no blue. There's only red and white. Go ahead and set them down. *(STUBBS keeps staring at the table, holding the toys in his hand.)*

WHITE WOMAN: We'd like a word with the manager, miss. Oh, miss!

WHITE MAN: She's completely ignoring us. *(One of the candles blows out.)*

GLORY BEE: Oh, shoot! *(GLORY BEE turns and heads back.)*

WHITE WOMAN: We'd like to speak to your manager.

GLORY BEE: Eat my socks. *(GLORY BEE exits right with the banana splits.)*

WHITE MAN: What'd she say?

COLONEL: Stubbs, get ahold of yourself. It's a simple equation. All we're trying to do is re-create a moment in time. A catastrophic moment in our personal history. That's all there is to it.

STUBBS *(holding figures)*: When I was hit—

COLONEL: No! Not that! *Not* when you were hit! We know all about that. We're fed up with that. We're up to here with that. It's the moment before. The exact moment *before* you were hit. That's the important moment here. Can't you get that through your thick head? Where were you standing in the battlefield? Where was my son?

STUBBS: Behind.

COLONEL *(pointing to a spot on table)*: Here?

STUBBS: Far away. Long ago. When they said—it would all be over.

COLONEL: Who said?

STUBBS: When they said it would all be done in a day.

COLONEL: Who?

STUBBS: Long, long ago. When they said he would be removed.

COLONEL: When who said who would be removed?

STUBBS: The enemy.

COLONEL: Where were you standing, Stubbs!

STUBBS: Far, far away.

COLONEL: I'm not talking about the location of the conflict! I'm talking about the battlefield itself! Where exactly were you on the field of battle!

STUBBS *(toasting his cup)*: LONG LIVE THE ENEMY!

COLONEL: Give me those soldiers! Give them back! *(STUBBS refuses and clutches the toys with both hands, close to his chest. Pause.)* You don't want me to take them back by force, do you, Stubbs? You don't want that. *(Pause. STUBBS slowly, reluctantly relinquishes the toy soldiers to the COLONEL. COLONEL places them on the table, then pulls STUBBS away from the table and propels the wheelchair into the wall upstage left.)* Now— Since you seem to find it so impossible to follow the simplest directions—to answer the simplest questions—I'm going to have to experiment here with various positions. Various, hypothetical arrangements—seemingly random but nevertheless with a comprehensive knowledge and background in hand-to-hand combat and military strategy. *(STUBBS abruptly wheels himself across the stage and exits.)* Stubbs! Get back over here! The situation has to be faced! *(STUBBS reenters from right.)*

STUBBS: I was here. Facing the green sea. I was smelling it. Through the smoke. It didn't smell American to me. It smelled like a foreign sea. The birds were not American birds. I wanted to have a feeling for home but nothing called me back. I wanted to have a memory. I prayed for a memory. But nothing came but smoke and the smell of dead fish.

COLONEL: Stubbs, we don't have a hope in hell of understanding the catastrophe if you're going to allow your mind to wander through smoke and dead fish! You've got to pull yourself together now! Grab ahold of your bootstraps! *(STUBBS blows his whistle and crosses to centerstage.)*

STUBBS: I was here!

COLONEL *(pointing at table)*: You were *here*! Caught in a cross fire!

STUBBS *(facing audience)*: I couldn't remember the faces—the voices—of the ones. I wanted to see them but their faces never came to me. Never came back.

COLONEL *(jabbing the table)*: We have to pinpoint the location!

STUBBS *(remaining centerstage)*: America had disappeared. *(COLONEL stands suddenly, in a fury, and draws his saber.)*

COLONEL *(saber drawn)*: DON'T TALK FOOLISHLY! That's a blasphemous thing to say! It's a disgrace to the memory of my son! I'm not buying dessert for anyone who makes a comment like that! The principles are enduring. You know that. This country wasn't founded on spineless, spur–of–the–moment whimsy. The effects are international! UNIVERSAL! *(COLONEL smashes his sword down on the table, upsetting all the toys. An explosion close by, offstage. Immediately the percussionists and war sounds join in full swing. The cyclorama explodes with bombs, missiles, and blown-up planes. This time, silhouetted against the panorama of light, stylized shapes of tanks, infantry, and heavy artillery move from right to left, in the heat of battle. GLORY BEE enters again, from right, balancing the two banana splits with an even larger candle burning in the center of each one. She makes her way slowly across the stage toward the red booth, all her attention riveted to the tray and the desserts. The "war" keeps raging behind her. When she finally reaches the booth she sets the banana splits down on the table. All the sounds, images, and effects suddenly stop. Silence. The COLONEL's gaze is fixed on the candles. STUBBS remains staring out over audience. Pause.)*

GLORY BEE: I hope the candles are all right, sir. That's all I could find in the kitchen.

COLONEL: Candles are fine.

GLORY BEE: We keep a supply on hand for the blackouts.

COLONEL: They're just fine.

GLORY BEE: Are you sure you don't want me to sing, sir? I'd be glad to sing.

COLONEL: No singing. Nobody was born today.

GLORY BEE: Is there going to be anything else, sir?

COLONEL: Not right now.

GLORY BEE: More coffee?

COLONEL: Yes, maybe some more of that.

GLORY BEE: I'll be right back. Enjoy your dessert.

COLONEL: Thank you so very much. (COLONEL *keeps staring at the candles as* GLORY BEE *crosses back to right.* STUBBS *stays center.* WHITE WOMAN *stops* GLORY BEE *as she passes.)*

WHITE WOMAN: Oh, miss!

GLORY BEE: Your clam chowder will be up any second now.

WHITE MAN: I don't want it. It's too late for clam chowder.

WHITE WOMAN: I would like to tell you something, miss.

GLORY BEE: Shoot.

WHITE WOMAN: Did you know that those two men over there are drinking hard liquor in your restaurant? Your family restaurant. *(Pause.* GLORY BEE *turns and looks at the* COLONEL.)

GLORY BEE *(back to* WHITE WOMAN): No, I didn't know that.

WHITE WOMAN: Well, they are. I watched them sneak it into their coffee. They're very sneaky, those two. I'd like to speak to your manager.

GLORY BEE: The manager is dead. *(GLORY BEE exits.)*

WHITE MAN: What'd she say?

WHITE WOMAN: I hope she realizes that I still want my clam chowder even though you don't want yours.

WHITE MAN: She realizes nothing. *(Pause. STUBBS wheels himself extreme downstage center and parks there, staring out at audience. COLONEL remains in booth, staring at candles. White couple resume their trance state.)*

COLONEL *(staring at candles)*: Stubbs? The dessert is here. It's arrived. *(Pause. No response from STUBBS. He just stares at audience.)* She remembered the candles. God bless her. *(STUBBS blows his whistle and suddenly lifts his shirt again, exposing his chest wound to the audience.)* Stubbs? I sincerely hope there hasn't been a serious breach created between us. I wouldn't want something like that. Not today, anyhow. We must remember why we came here. We can't forget our purpose. Stubbs? *(Pause. STUBBS remains with his shirt up. No response.)* Are you with me on this? Look—I'll drop the whole business about the specific positions. I know it irritates you. I'll drop that. I promise you. Important as it may be for our— *(Pause. COLONEL stares at STUBBS who remains as before. No response.)* It was simply a means of finding some common ground, Stubbs. *(Pause. No response from STUBBS.)* All right, look—I'll put all the toys away. How's that suit you? If you're going to be a baby about it. *(COLONEL begins to clear the table of all the toys and puts them back in his bag. He keeps speaking through all this. STUBBS remains with his shirt up, facing front. Collecting toys.)* See? I'm putting the toys away, Stubbs! They're disappearing one by one. You don't have to worry about any of that. Out of sight, out of mind! All I want— All I've ever wanted was for us to toast the death of my son and have a nice dessert. That's all. Simple as that. Stubbs?

STUBBS *(still holding up his shirt)*: God bless the enemy!

COLONEL: There's no reason in this wide world to put a wall up between us. That's not going to get us anywhere. What was it I said, anyway? What was it, specifically, that I said that could have caused this cruel reaction? All I said was: "Don't talk foolishly." That's all. "Don't talk foolishly." I could have said that to anyone. I could have said it to myself. In fact, I may very well have been referring to myself when I said that. It wasn't even directed at you. It was directed at me. I heard how foolish I was sounding and I made that comment and then you went and took it personally, as though I were referring to something you said when, in fact, it was something I said. *(Pause.* STUBBS *remains with his shirt up. No response. Silence.)* I suppose now what we're going to do is forget all that time in the hospital. Is that it? All that long time when I nursed you. Changed your shitty sheets. Cleaned your fingernails? Emptied your bladder bag. You don't remember any of that, I suppose. That's all been long forgot. *(Pause. Slowly,* STUBBS *lowers his shirt and stares out at audience.)*

STUBBS *(quietly, facing out)*: I remember the moment you forsook me. The moment you gave me up.

COLONEL: That dog won't hunt, Stubbs. There was never anything like that and you know it. We've been through all this before. Now come and eat your dessert.

STUBBS: The moment you invented my death.

COLONEL: I'm going to start without you in a minute!

STUBBS: When you threw me away. *(COLONEL suddenly throws a fit and starts beating on the table with his fist, then, just as suddenly, he stops.)*

COLONEL *(slamming table)*: I NEVER, NEVER, NEVER, NEVER!!!!! *(Explosion with short burst of percussion.* STUBBS *keeps staring out at audience.)*

STUBBS *(facing front)*: When you left me it went straight through me and out the other side. It left a hole I can never fill. *(Pause. Silence.)*

COLONEL: Stubbs. Please. I don't want to eat alone. Not today. It makes no sense. Any other day I'd be glad to eat alone, even welcomed it. I've loved to eat alone. I've gone out of my way to eat alone. I've walked miles in search of empty restaurants. You know that. But not today. The purpose of all this was to honor my dead son. We have to do it together.

STUBBS *(facing out)*: Someone was killed. But it wasn't me. I'm not the one. *(STUBBS wheels himself over to the booth and parks in front of his banana split.)* I'm the lucky one.

COLONEL: Good. That's good. As long as we can always come back to our senses. That's the important thing. It's a blessing, Stubbs. It's a gift. An American virtue. As far out on a limb as circumstances might shove us we always have that possibility of returning to our common sense. Our fairness. Even in the midst of the most horrible devastation. Under the most terrible kind of duress. Torture. Barbarism of all sorts. Starvation. Chemical warfare. Public hangings. Mutilation of children. Raping of mothers. Raping of daughters. Raping of brothers and fathers. Executions of entire families. Entire generations of families. Amputation of private organs. Decapitation. Disembowelment. Dismemberment. Disinturnment. Eradication of wildlife. You name it. We can't forget that we were generated from the bravest stock. The Pioneer. The Mountain Man. The Plainsman. The Texas Ranger. The Lone Ranger. My son. These have not died in vain. These ones have not left us to wallow in various states of insanity and self-abuse. We have a legacy to continue, Stubbs. It's up to us. No one else is going to do it for us. Here's to them and to my son! A soldier for his nation! *(They toast and click their cups.)*

COLONEL *and* STUBBS: THE ENEMY HAS BROUGHT US TOGETHER! *(COLONEL blows out the candles.)*

COLONEL *(picking up spoon)*: Let's dig in, Stubbs. *(COLONEL begins to eat with gusto, but STUBBS just stares at his dessert. GLORY BEE enters from right, very slowly again, balancing two bowls of clam chowder on her tray, making her way carefully toward the white couple.)*

WHITE WOMAN: Here she comes.

WHITE MAN: Is that our order?

WHITE WOMAN: I think it's finally us.

WHITE MAN: But I don't want mine. Didn't she understand that?

WHITE WOMAN: She understands nothing.

WHITE MAN: It's too late for clam chowder. *(GLORY BEE reaches their table and sets a bowl down in front of each of them.)*

GLORY BEE: Here we go. Sorry for the delay, but the cook has been wounded.

WHITE WOMAN: There's no excuse.

WHITE MAN: Didn't you understand that I don't want mine?

GLORY BEE: I thought you were just saying that.

WHITE MAN: Saying what?

GLORY BEE: That you didn't want yours.

WHITE MAN: That's what I did say.

WHITE WOMAN: He did say that. I heard him.

GLORY BEE: I heard him too.

WHITE WOMAN: So why'd you bring it when you heard him say it?

WHITE MAN: It's too late for clam chowder. The time has passed. (GLORY BEE *dumps bowl of clam chowder in* WHITE MAN'S *lap, then throws the bowl offstage right. A loud crash of dishes follows.* WHITE WOMAN *eats her clam chowder.*)

GLORY BEE: Will there be anything else, sir? (GLORY BEE *exits right.*)

WHITE WOMAN (*eating*): What'd she do?

COLONEL: Eat your banana split, Stubbs. It's going to get all runny. (STUBBS *just stares at the dessert.* COLONEL *continues to eat.* WHITE WOMAN *continues to eat.* WHITE MAN, *after staring at his lap for a while, begins to wipe the mess up with his napkin. As he eats.*) You're not still pouting, are you? Holding some kind of secret grudge? (*Pause.* STUBBS *keeps staring at his dessert.*) I don't know what ever gave you this idea that I would have deliberately deceived you. Where did you come up with a notion like that? Who put that in your noggin? (*Pause.* STUBBS *keeps staring.* WHITE MAN *keeps cleaning. Still eating.*) You don't think for a minute that if you actually were my son that I would dream up this elaborate scheme, do you? What would be the purpose of that? Where would that get us? (*Suddenly* STUBBS *smashes his banana split with his fist. Everyone else continues as usual.*)

STUBBS: I'M EIGHTY PERCENT MUTILATED!!!!!

COLONEL: Nothing to be done about that, Stubbs. All in the past. Can't wallow in our miseries. Now you've gone and ruined a perfectly good dessert. Suppose you think I'm going to buy you another one. Well, you're dead wrong about that. Just because you've burnt the bacon doesn't mean *I* drink the grease. (*The* WHITE MAN'S *cleaning of his lap slowly turns into masturbation as* WHITE WOMAN *continues eating, oblivious.*) That's what comes from striking out blindly. Have to learn to pay for your actions. Become a man.

STUBBS: Become a man.

COLONEL: Exactly. *(STUBBS turns his wheelchair toward WHITE MAN and moves toward him, then stops. He blows his whistle. WHITE MAN continues masturbating. WHITE WOMAN keeps eating.)*

STUBBS *(to WHITE MAN)*: Become a man!

COLONEL *(continuing to eat)*: Clean up your mess now, Stubbs. Don't leave it for someone else. *(STUBBS keeps staring at WHITE MAN who continues getting more worked up as WHITE WOMAN ignores him.)*

STUBBS *(to WHITE MAN)*: BECOME A MAN!

COLONEL: Stubbs! Get back over here and clean up your mess or I'm going to have to spank you! Do you want a good spanking? Is that what you want? A good solid thrashing. Maybe that's what you need.

STUBBS *(to WHITE MAN)*: BECOME A MAN! *(WHITE MAN continues, carrying himself to the verge of orgasm.)*

COLONEL *(standing)*: All right! All right! You leave me no alternative. *(COLONEL unbuckles his sword and lays it on the table. He crosses, downstage, opening his jacket and removing his belt as he goes. WHITE MAN keeps masturbating through this and gradually reaches a climax as WHITE WOMAN continues to eat. Circling STUBBS with belt.)* I do my damnedest to appeal to your good sense and reason. I bend over backward and where does it get me? You throw it all back in my face. You blatantly refuse me. Your arrogance is a slander on all that I stand for. All that I've slaved for. It's not just me, Stubbs. It's the principles. The codes. The entire infrastructure that you cast aspersions on. When I thrash you, you must remember this. You must hold it in your mind when you feel the sting of the whip. You must keep it at the most forefront of your consciousness. You must never forget that your punishment has a purpose. LONG LIVE THE ENEMY! (COLONEL *begins to savagely whip* STUBBS *with the belt. In the course of this,* WHITE MAN *reaches orgasm.* STUBBS *is beaten to the floor, but* COLONEL *continues, relentlessly.)*

STUBBS: LONG LIVE THE ENEMY! (*As the beating continues, the cyclorama is again lit up with the fireworks of war. The drummers erupt from backstage.* STUBBS *crawls around the stage on all fours as* COLONEL *pummels him with the belt. The* WHITE WOMAN *continues eating calmly through all this.* WHITE MAN *slumps in his chair, exhausted.* STUBBS *finally collapses in a heap with* COLONEL *standing over him. The war panorama subsides. Sounds and drums fade. Pause as* COLONEL *puts his belt back on but remains over* STUBBS. GLORY BEE *enters from right again with a pot of coffee on her tray, crossing very slowly toward the booth, completely focused on the coffeepot. Silence.)*

COLONEL (*to* GLORY BEE *as she passes behind him*): If you stare at the pot, you're bound to spill. (GLORY BEE *keeps steadfastly making her way to the booth. When she gets there she refills the two cups.)* I'm going to give you another chance, Stubbs. One last chance. God knows I've given you enough already. We're going to go back in time. You and me. Back to the field of battle. We're going to fix ourselves there just as surely as though we were standing there today. Breathing the fire. Staring straight into the eyeballs of death itself. (COLONEL *stands and crosses back to the booth, leaving* STUBBS *on the floor.)*

STUBBS (*on floor*): From here I can see their boots. (COLONEL *reaches the booth and picks up the toy infantrymen.)*

GLORY BEE (*to* COLONEL): Did you make this mess?

COLONEL: No. He˙ did. (COLONEL *crosses back to* STUBBS *with the toys and squats next to him on the floor. He sets the toys down.* STUBBS *stares at the toys.)*

STUBBS: From here, I can see their bodies mixed with ours.

COLONEL: Sit up now, Stubbs, and take stock of things.

STUBBS *(still lying on the floor)*: Their heads are blown off. *(COLONEL spanks STUBBS hard on his ass.)*

COLONEL: SIT UP, I SAID! *(STUBBS pulls himself to a sitting position, facing the toys.)*

STUBBS: Some of their heads have fallen on the bodies of our own men. It's a funny sight. *(COLONEL slaps STUBBS across the face.)*

COLONEL: SNAP OUT OF IT!

WHITE WOMAN: Give it to him! You should have done that when he was just a little boy. All of this could have been avoided. *(COLONEL crouches closer to STUBBS and becomes more confidential. GLORY BEE is cleaning up the banana split mess at the booth.)*

COLONEL: It's the loss, Stubbs. The loss. That's what puzzles me. How could we be so victorious and still suffer this terrible loss? How could that be? Was it an accident? A stray piece of shrapnel that broke off and tore through his chest? That doesn't seem fair, does it? Here you are, still alive. Living the lush life, having a dessert. And he's gone. Vanished. Blown to tiny pieces. There wasn't even enough left of him to bury a finger. I asked them to send me a finger. A toe. A strand of his hair. They couldn't find the slightest trace. Not even a scrap of flesh. *(GLORY BEE suddenly starts singing an old Billie Holiday song in full voice as she cleans up the banana split mess. She sings with real feeling, not trying to parody the lyrics. All the other characters are suspended.)*

GLORY BEE *(singing)*:
Good morning heart-ache
Here we go again
Good morning heart-ache
You're the one who knew me when

Might as well get used to you
Hangin' around
Good morning heart-ache
Sit down.
(She exits with tray and coffeepot, right. This time she moves quickly and freely with no concern about spilling. Pause. STUBBS *and* COLONEL *are staring out at audience. Silence.)*

COLONEL: What time is it? What am I thinking? *(*COLONEL *stands abruptly, digging an old railroad pocket watch out of his coat and checking the time. He turns around himself as though suddenly lost.* STUBBS *remains on the floor.)* What am I thinking, Stubbs? We have to get you back before the curfew. Where's my sword? What's become of my sword? *(He sees his sword lying on the table by the booth and moves toward it, then stops suddenly and turns back to* STUBBS.*)* Your pills! The pills! You haven't taken your pills! *(*COLONEL *starts patting all his coat pockets, searching for a bottle of pills as he moves back to* STUBBS.*)* You haven't taken them yet, have you, Stubbs? Try to remember. *(*STUBBS *is busy moving the toy soldiers around on the floor, placing them in positions.* COLONEL *keeps turning in small, nervous circles, patting and searching through his jacket.)* What am I thinking? What the hell am I thinking? I know I brought them with me. I remember picking them up off your side table. I remember having a sense of duty about it. *(*COLONEL *finally finds the bottle of pills in one of his pockets.)* Aha! I knew it! I knew I hadn't forgotten. Thank God! Thank Christ! Thank the Holy Ghost! I have them, Stubbs! I have them right here. *(*COLONEL *moves right and yells offstage for* GLORY BEE. STUBBS *keeps maneuvering the toys. Yelling off right.)* Oh, miss! Miss! What the hell was her name? "Bee" somebody? Miss! A glass of water, please! It's an emergency! *(*COLONEL *returns to* STUBBS *and brings the wheelchair over next to him.)* Come on now, Stubbs. We have to get you back before they lock the doors on us. We'll be up shit creek without a paddle.

STUBBS (*on floor with toys*): It's very clear what happened. We were back to back. Like this. (*He moves toys.*) Exactly like this.

COLONEL: Stubbs, get up off the floor now. You have to take your pills.

STUBBS: Caught in a cross fire.

COLONEL: STUBBS!

STUBBS: Don't yell at me. That'll get you nowhere.

COLONEL: Please, Stubbs. Take your pills now. We have to get you back or they'll suspend my visiting privileges. They're very strict about that. You know how they are.

STUBBS: I could feel his spine trembling on my spine. There was nothing we could do about fear. We couldn't bargain with fear. We couldn't talk ourselves out of it. Neither one of us knew how to pray. We had no idea who God was. Who was God? (COLONEL *picks up* STUBBS *and puts him back into the wheelchair.*)

COLONEL: We can reconstruct this later. At the hospital. We'll have all day tomorrow. We have all week.

STUBBS: It was friendly fire that took us out. That's what it was. You could see it heading at us from the mountain, not the sea. It was coming straight at us.

COLONEL: If they lock the doors on us, Stubbs, we'll be sitting ducks. We'll be on the street. Wide open to attack.

STUBBS: It was friendly fire. It smiled in my face. I could see its teeth when it hit us. I could see its tongue.

COLONEL: Pull yourself together now, Stubbs! We're going to have to make a sprint for it! If we're caught in the open they'll cut us to pieces! (STUBBS *faces audience in wheelchair as*

GLORY BEE *enters, from right, very slowly, balancing a glass of water on her tray and moving inch by inch toward* STUBBS.)

STUBBS: There was a face on the nose of the missile. They'd painted a face. You could see it coming. A lizard with smiling teeth. A friendly lizard. It was seeking us out. Hunting our warm bodies. It was glad it found us. You could tell. It was happy to receive us. It could care less who we were, but happy we were human. Happy we weren't just a concrete bunker or another stupid building. Overjoyed that we had skin and blood. We opened our arms to it. We couldn't resist its embrace. We were lovers when it hit us. We were in heaven. (COLONEL *crosses to* GLORY BEE *with the bottle of pills in his hand. He stops her.*)

COLONEL *(to* GLORY BEE): Can't you remember the simplest thing! Don't stare at the glass! You're bound to spill if you stare at the glass. I've told you that a thousand times. Here, let me show you. (COLONEL *tries to take the tray and glass away from* GLORY BEE, *but she won't give it up. Pulling tray.*) Give it to me! Release your hold! (GLORY BEE *releases her grip and* COLONEL *takes it. He begins to move randomly around the stage, balancing the glass on the tray. He spins and turns, leaps in the air, making a ridiculous dance out of his demonstration as* GLORY BEE *watches.* STUBBS *stares straight out, ignoring the* COLONEL. *To* GLORY BEE.) Now watch me. Study it closely. (*He begins to dance.*) You have to pick a point in space. A specific point. Sometimes it's helpful to close one eye until you've found it. One eye may be more dominant than the other, in which case you have to experiment. You have to test them for accuracy and precision, always bearing in mind your ultimate objective. Your specific mission. Always reminding yourself that the human body is little more than a complex machine and, like all machines, can be trained and programmed to fulfill our every need. Through repetition and practice. Repetition and practice. Slowly, a pattern begins to emerge. Slowly, through my own diligence and perseverance, this pattern takes on a beauty and form that would have otherwise been incomprehensible to my random, chaotic laziness. Now I become a master of my own destiny. I can see the writing on the wall. I understand my purpose in the grand scheme of things. There's no longer any doubt. Fear takes a backseat to the certainty and confidence that now consumes my entire being. I am a God among men! I move in a different sphere. I fly on the wings of my own initiative! *(COLONEL spins to a stop and turns toward GLORY BEE. To GLORY BEE.)* You see? How simple? How pure? Now, you try it. *(COLONEL moves toward GLORY BEE, holding out the tray and glass of water to her. She refuses to take it.)* Here. Give it a whirl. It's your turn now. *(GLORY BEE refuses.)* You don't want a beating, do you?

WHITE WOMAN: You'd better try it. I've seen him when he comes apart and it's not a pretty sight.

COLONEL *(to GLORY BEE)*: Maybe you'd like a good beating. *(GLORY BEE takes the tray and glass reluctantly as COLONEL escorts her downstage left by the arm. STUBBS blows his whistle and lifts his shirt again, showing his scar to the audience. COLONEL grabs one side of GLORY'S tray so that the two of them are holding it between them, balancing the glass of water. To GLORY BEE.)* Now—simply let yourself go and allow your body to give itself up to the force of my superior momentum. Here we go. Cast your fate to the wind! *(COLONEL begins to propel GLORY BEE around the stage. They move like a dance team with GLORY BEE falling right into the rhythm. WHITE MAN begins to sing as COLONEL and GLORY BEE waltz to the melody, holding the tray and glass between them.)*

WHITE MAN *(singing)*:
Sometimes I live in the country
Sometimes I live in the town
Sometimes I have a great notion
To jump into the river and drown

Irene, good night
Irene, good night
Good night, Irene
Good night, Irene
I'll see you in my dreams.

WHITE MAN *and* WHITE WOMAN *(singing)*:
Last Saturday night I got married
Me and my wife settled down
Now me and my wife are parted
I'm gonna take another stroll downtown

Irene, good night
Irene, good night
Good night, Irene
Good night, Irene
I'll see you in my dreams.©

*(*COLONEL *and* GLORY BEE *continue their dance all over the stage.)*

COLONEL *(waltzing)*: Stubbs, I think I'm in love. Do you think
that's possible? At my late age? *(*STUBBS *pulls his shirt back
down and stares straight ahead as* COLONEL *and* GLORY BEE
continue to waltz.)

STUBBS: No.

COLONEL: You're only jealous, Stubbs. You're maimed and jealous. It's a shame.

STUBBS: MY THING HANGS LIKE DEAD MEAT!

COLONEL *(dancing)*: Exactly. No son of mine has a "thing" like
that. It's not possible.

STUBBS: If my "thing" comes back. If it grows straight and strong
and tall— Will you take me back?

COLONEL: Too late for that, Stubbs. The time has passed. On the
other hand, things are looking up for me.

STUBBS: You're in love.

COLONEL: Exactly.

STUBBS: Suddenly.

COLONEL: Right.

STUBBS: She's caused you to forget the curfew.

COLONEL: That's correct.

STUBBS: She's caused you to forget my pills.

COLONEL: We're running away to Mexico!

STUBBS: You're leaving me for good?

COLONEL: Exactly. It's a dead end, Stubbs. We did our best. Here. Take your pills. You might as well take them. *(COLONEL dances GLORY BEE over to STUBBS and sets the tray, glass, and pills down on STUBBS's lap, then dances off again with GLORY BEE in his arms.)*

STUBBS: IT'S TOO LATE FOR PILLS! *(STUBBS throws the tray, glass, and pills off right. A loud crash of dishes follows, off right, more like an explosion.)*

COLONEL *(still dancing)*: That's not the attitude we try to engender, Stubbs. It's only the present that stinks. Try to remember that. The future holds bright promise. Acapulco! Marimbas under the full moon! A new name! I was thinking something along the lines of: "Mr. and Mrs. Domingo Chalupas." We'd be entirely incognito. A mystery surrounds us! We begin to spawn children. All boys! Each of them physically perfect in their own way. Each of them beyond reproach. It's not too late to begin again, and with a woman like this, the prospects are endless!

STUBBS: Will you miss me?

COLONEL: I may have moments, Stubbs. A moment here, a moment there. Fleeting moments.

STUBBS: But you'll try to forget me? To wipe me out?

COLONEL: I'll do my best.

STUBBS: You'll never erase me completely.

COLONEL: Don't be so sure about that.

STUBBS: You'll miss the Enemy.

COLONEL: I'll make a new one. I'm very adaptable.

STUBBS: You'll never replace me.

COLONEL (still dancing): It's already been done!

STUBBS: She'll never hold up to the punishment!

COLONEL: She's a woman of substance.

STUBBS: She'll bottom out!

COLONEL: Not a chance.

STUBBS: She'll wish she'd never been born!

COLONEL: Bitterness, Stubbs. Bitterness.

STUBBS: Why are you so determined to abandon me? Is it my HELPLESSNESS! (STUBBS suddenly stands on wobbly legs, trying desperately to keep his balance. COLONEL and GLORY BEE stop dancing and stare at him. Pause.)

COLONEL: Stubbs. Don't be an idiot! (STUBBS falls back into the wheelchair, breathing hard from the struggle to stand. Pause.)

STUBBS: Is it my IMPOTENCE! (STUBBS stands again, gripping an arm of the wheelchair, then letting go and tottering badly as though about to fall flat on his face.)

COLONEL: There are certain things that are irreversible, Stubbs. Irreversible. Now, sit down and stop trying to be a hero. You're less pathetic as a cripple. (STUBBS begins to fall forward. GLORY BEE rushes to him and props him up before he has a chance to fall. STUBBS remains standing at an angle with most of his weight being supported by GLORY BEE, who groans under the effort. COLO-

NEL *makes no move to help.)* This won't change anything, Stubbs. This sad little last-ditch attempt. It won't change a heartbeat. It certainly won't bring my son back, now, will it? *(STUBBS throws his arms around GLORY BEE's shoulders and begins to stagger forward haphazardly toward left with GLORY BEE still trying to support him.)*

STUBBS: Your son. *Your* son. I remember him running. Crazy. Running toward the beach. Throwing his rifle in the green sea. Throwing his arms to the sky. Running to the mountain. Back to the beach. Screaming. I remember his eyes.

GLORY BEE *(supporting STUBBS)*: I can't keep this up forever, you know. I'm a waitress.

STUBBS: I remember his eyes. *(STUBBS and GLORY BEE stop, left, but she remains supporting his weight. COLONEL moves to the wheelchair.)*

COLONEL: We're bound to miss curfew now, Stubbs. I hope you're proud of yourself. I hope you're good and happy about that.

STUBBS: I remember him falling. Picking him up. Dragging him down the beach. Screaming his head off. Carrying him on my back. *(STUBBS staggers forward with GLORY BEE supporting him desperately.)*

GLORY BEE: Oh, my God.

STUBBS: He kept speaking your name in my ear. Whispering it. Chanting your name like a prayer. Calling to you as though you might appear out of nowhere.

GLORY BEE *(staggering under his weight)*: This is pure torture, you know. *(STUBBS continues to stagger, with GLORY BEE doing her best to keep him upright.)*

COLONEL: What're you going to do when she finds out about your "thing," Stubbs? How're you going to explain that one?

STUBBS: As though you might suddenly appear and save him. Transport him back across the green sea. Sweep him up in your arms and take him safely back home.

GLORY BEE: I can't hold you forever, you know.

STUBBS *(continuing to stagger)*: Keep thinking of "home." That's the way to pull through this. Fix a picture in your mind. A backyard. A tree house. A better time. Truman, maybe. "Straight-Talkin' Harry." Think of station wagons! County Fairs! Ferris Wheels! Think of canned goods and cotton candy! Home Economics. Production lines! The Great Northern Railroad! Think of what we've achieved! The "Trail of Tears"! The Mississippi! Samuel Clemens! Little Richard! The Dust Bowl! The Gold Rush! The Natchez Trace! It's endless! A River of Victory in all directions! Flooding the Plains! Hold to an image! Lock onto a picture of glorious, unending expansion! DON'T LET YOURSELF SLIP INTO DOUBT!! Don't let it happen! You'll be swallowed whole!

GLORY BEE: I can't keep this up!

STUBBS *(staggering badly)*: Lock onto an image or you'll be blown to KINGDOM COME!! *(STUBBS and GLORY BEE crash headlong onto the booth and lie there in a pile, exhausted and breathing hard. COLONEL pushes the wheelchair over near the booth, then slowly sits down in it. Pause.)*

COLONEL: All right, Stubbs. Have it your way. Looks like we've finally hit our crossroads here. I may just have to make a dash for the hospital on my own bat. Completely unassisted. Is that what it's come down to? A final split? An absolute parting of the ways? *(Pause. STUBBS and GLORY BEE just lie there, breathing hard. COLONEL turns the wheelchair and wheels himself away from the booth, very slowly, almost leisurely, toward downstage right. GLORY BEE props herself up and looks out into space. Pause.)*

GLORY BEE *(in booth)*: You know what I miss? You remember how we used to have those little "quiet times" just before the sirens? Way back when it first started? I think it's a shame we don't have those anymore.

WHITE MAN: I agree.

GLORY BEE: I miss those so much.

WHITE WOMAN: I don't remember any "quiet time." When was that?

WHITE MAN: You remember. *(COLONEL arrives downstage right in wheelchair and stops, staring out over audience. Pause.)*

COLONEL: Maybe you think you're breaking my heart with this desperate show of independence. But don't get excited. I was born in isolation. If I can't have companionship it won't kill me. Aggression is the only answer. A man needs a good hobby. Something he can sink his teeth into. *(STUBBS sits up, clutching at the booth for support. GLORY BEE stays seated in the booth. COLONEL remains sitting in wheelchair, facing audience.)*

STUBBS *(quietly, to COLONEL)*: I remember the moment you forsook me. The moment you invented my death. That moment has lasted all my life.

COLONEL *(facing front)*: Your imagination has done you in, Stubbs. If you think you're breaking my heart, you're sadly mistaken. I can easily do without. It's a question of training. Repetition and practice. Repetition and practice. All those days. All those horrible long days without the enemy. Longing out the window. Staring at the stupid boredom of peacetime. The dullness of it. The idiot deadness in everyone's eyes. Did you think I was just treading water back then? Spinning my wheels? I was gearing up, Stubbs. Silently stockpiling my secret arsenal for just such an occasion as this. Knowing full well that the enemy has the same hunger for me as I have for him. Never doubting for a second that he

would reemerge. He would reemerge because I com-
manded it.

GLORY BEE *(from booth)*: The thing I can't get over is, it never
occurred to me that "Danny's" could be invaded. I always
thought we were invulnerable to attack. The landscaping.
The lighting. The parking lot. All the pretty bushes. Who
could touch us? Who would dare?

WHITE MAN: I absolutely agree.

GLORY BEE *(from booth)*: When the first wave of missiles hit us I
kept studying the menu. I thought the menu would save me
somehow. The pretty colored photographs of all our spe-
cials. The "Catfish Dinner." The "Chicken-Fried Steak." I
worshipped the menu.

WHITE MAN: What was it we used to do in those "quiet times"?

WHITE WOMAN: You got me.

WHITE MAN: Didn't we dance or something? Weren't we on a
pier? A dock of some kind? Watching lights in the distance?

WHITE WOMAN: Have you lost your mind?

WHITE MAN: Didn't we dance cheek to cheek?

WHITE WOMAN: COME TO YOUR SENSES! *(She whacks the*
WHITE MAN *across the head with her purse. He doesn't react. An*
explosion in the distance.)

COLONEL *(in wheelchair, facing front)*: If you think you can touch
me in some way—fondle me—cajole me into your frame of
reference— If you think you can make an appeal of some
kind—maybe beg—maybe crawl and pray—maybe sacrifice
your own blood or the blood of your children. You're sadly
mistaken. *(Suddenly, from left, a metal busboy's wagon, loaded*
with gas masks, is rolled onstage. It arrives all by itself and stops
centerstage. The characters ignore it. Pause.)

GLORY BEE: I worshipped the menu. To me it held a life. An unthreatened life. Better than the Bible. I missed the Cold War with all my heart.

WHITE MAN: Me too.

COLONEL: I think she senses your weakness, Stubbs. She can smell it on you. How could she help but smell it? The hole through your middle. The rotting core. The limpness. There's no way you can disguise something like that. Your only hope is to throw yourself at my feet and beg for mercy. Imitate my every move. I'm your only chance now.

WHITE WOMAN: Shouldn't we be getting under the table by now? Shouldn't we be tucking our heads between our knees? (STUBBS *stands again, suddenly.*)

STUBBS: If we can make it to the mountain, they might realize we're on the same side! We'll wave every flag we can get our hands on. Every color. They've got to recognize us! (STUBBS *lurches forward, losing his balance as he heads upstage.* GLORY BEE *stays sitting in the booth and watches* STUBBS *as he crashes headlong into the metal wagon, upsetting all the gas masks. He falls and just lies there.* COLONEL *continues to sit in wheelchair, staring out over audience without turning back toward* STUBBS *and his accident. Pause.*)

COLONEL: A touching display. I still think Mexico is the ticket, when you get right down to it. (GLORY BEE *kneels down next to* STUBBS *and strokes his back softly but mechanically.*)

GLORY BEE: I missed the sounds of people clinking coffee cups. Spoons scraping on bowls. Knives and forks scratching plates. The rustle of napkins and money.

COLONEL (*still facing audience*): She's playing you for a sucker, Stubbs. You can see right through it.

GLORY BEE: I missed the voices of conversations I couldn't make out. Just the sounds of humans temporarily stopping for breakfast, then moving on.

COLONEL: Tell her about your "thing," Stubbs! Don't forget about that. Best to get it out in the open. (STUBBS *rolls over on his back and embraces* GLORY BEE, *pulling her on top of him.*)

STUBBS (*rolling with* GLORY BEE, *holding her*): Lock onto a picture of "home."

COLONEL (*still facing front but getting worried*): Now, listen to me, Stubbs! Let's not fly off the handle here. The truth of it is that we may, in fact, be somehow remotely related. I'm not saying directly, now. I'm not at all suggesting first genera-tion or anything like that. But possibly cousins. Second cousins at the very least. It's within the realm of possibility. There's certain evidence that I've withheld until I was sure I'd gathered all the facts. I didn't want you to become overexcited for no good reason. (STUBBS *rolls across the floor with* GLORY BEE *held in his grip.* COLONEL *spins the wheelchair around, facing* STUBBS. *Directly to* STUBBS.) Stubbs! Don't be a maniac! Give that up! Give it all up! Relinquish your self completely! If you promise me this— If you make a solemn oath—Scout's honor. Hope to die. Stick a needle in your eye. If you give me some sign of total, absolute, uncondi-tional submission—then I might—I just might consider— *adopting* you. I'm serious, Stubbs. I'm absolutely serious. I'll fill out the necessary forms. I'll go through all the red tape. I don't mind a bit. But only if you swear on a stack of Bibles to submit!

STUBBS (*rolling on floor with* GLORY BEE): My thing is coming back!

GLORY BEE: Oh, great! (COLONEL *propels the wheelchair quickly toward* STUBBS *and* GLORY BEE *as they continue to roll back and forth as one body.*)

COLONEL: That's not possible, Stubbs! That's out of the question. You have no say in the matter. It's already been decided long ago. It's a question of destiny!

WHITE WOMAN: Well, I'm not waiting anymore. At a certain point you have to take things into your own hands. (WHITE WOMAN *gets up from her chair, crosses to one of the gas masks on the floor, and picks it up. She returns to the table and puts the gas mask on.*)

STUBBS: My thing is arising! I can feel it!

COLONEL: Stubbs! Stubbs, you have to listen now. Your "thing" is not the issue. Your "thing" is beside the point. It has little consequence. It's a selfish, stupid, little tiny concern. Listen up!

STUBBS: It's coming back! It's all coming back to me now!

COLONEL: You're dreaming, Stubbs! Wildly hallucinating again.

STUBBS: No—listen—here's how it was. Listen to me now! (STUBBS *stops rolling with* GLORY BEE *and tries to sit up from the floor. He gets* GLORY BEE *to help him.* COLONEL *stays in wheelchair. Struggling to sit.*) When I was hit. It went straight through me and out—

COLONEL: We've heard that old song a thousand times.

STUBBS (*blowing his whistle loudly*): LISTEN TO ME! (COLONEL *stops and turns the wheelchair to face* STUBBS *from a distance. Pause. To* GLORY BEE.) Help me up. Help me get up! (GLORY BEE *pulls* STUBBS *up to his knees. Struggling to get to his knees.*) The part I remember— The part that's coming back—is this. (*To* COLONEL, *on his knees.*) Your face. Your face leaning over my face. Peering down.

COLONEL (*in wheelchair*): I was there. It's true. Right by your side.

STUBBS: Your face, lying. Smiling and lying. Your bald face of denial. Peering down from a distance. Bombing me.

COLONEL: I brought you everything you asked for! Powdered donuts. I went blocks out of my way to find them. Cracker

Jacks! Did you think they had those things in the cafeteria? Is that what you thought?

STUBBS: I remember your squirming silence.

COLONEL: I emptied your bladder bag!

STUBBS: You had my name changed! YOU INVENTED MY DEATH!

COLONEL: That simply isn't true, Stubbs. There was some mix-up. Some computer scramble. I don't know where you get these ideas.

STUBBS: No "next of kin." No "next of kin." A "friend of the family," they told me. That's what they told me!

COLONEL: It was simpler all the way around.

STUBBS: Some mysterious "friend of the family." A friend of a friend of my father's friend.

COLONEL: I was there from dawn 'til dusk. I watched the sun rise and fall on your stupid head! I listened to you babble. I read you comic books. *(Pause.)*

STUBBS *(on his knees)*: Your face of pure guilt. Squirming. Nothing to be done about that. No way of tracing it. Tracking it down. No way of knowing the original moment. Abraham, maybe. Maybe Abraham. Judas. Eve. Maybe her. No way of knowing for sure. Best way is to kill all the sons. Wipe them off the face of the earth. Bleed them of all their blood. Let it pour down into the soil. Let it fill every river. Every hole in this earth. Let it pour through every valley. Flood every town. Let us drown in the blood of our own. Let us drown and drink it. Let us go down screaming in the blood of our sons. *(COLONEL slowly wheels himself to downstage center, where he sits, facing out toward audience.)*

COLONEL: We've got to keep our back to the mountain, Stubbs. At all costs. You can see our position. We've got a perfect

vantage point from here. We're lucky in that respect. There
are certain advantages to isolation. After all, we're not in
exile. This is our domain. We've earned every inch of it.
Surrounded by water. Engulfed by the prairies. Marooned.
(Pause.) MAROOOOOOOOONED!! *(Pause.* GLORY BEE
picks up a gas mask and puts it on STUBBS, *then dons one herself
and curls into fetal position upstage center. The* WHITE MAN
*remains sitting in his chair, facing right without his gas mask on.
The* COLONEL *remains in wheelchair, facing out and not looking
back at* STUBBS.*)* It's the perfect situation. We couldn't have
asked for a better deal. If they attack us on our flank, we've
got them surrounded. If they come from air, sea, or land,
we'll cut them off at the pass. We're invincible, Stubbs.
There's no doubt about it. Invincible! *(*STUBBS *begins to rise
to his feet.)* Stubbs? You're right behind me, aren't you?
You're right where I imagine you to be? You're not turning
tail? Burying your face in the sand? Crying for mother? Put
your back up against me, Stubbs, so I can feel you. Press
your spine into my spine. Give me the impression that
you're with me to the bitter end. That's the spirit! *(Pause.*
STUBBS *is now standing and facing the back of the wheelchair.)*
Stubbs? We have to stick together in this. The sacrifice
needs a partner. You understand that, don't you? *(*STUBBS
begins to slowly advance on the COLONEL *from behind.)* The
attack could come at any second now. Put your back up
against me, Stubbs, so I can feel your spine. We're in this
together. *(*STUBBS *stands behind the wheelchair, staring down at
the* COLONEL'*s head, with his gas mask on.)* Stubbs? Are you
there? Are you still there? Don't run out on me now. As
soon as this is over, I'll take you back. I promise you. I will.
I'll make it official. Lock, stock, and barrel. It's not too late
for that. I'll proclaim it in public. *(Pause.)* Stubbs? Are you
listening? You haven't left me yet? You haven't disappeared? STUBBS! *(Suddenly,* STUBBS *grabs the* COLONEL
around the neck in a stranglehold. Choking, in STUBBS'*s stranglehold.)* If you're very good, Stubbs— If you're very, very

good—I'll buy you two desserts. Anything you want. Hot fudge. Milky Ways. Anything your heart desires. I'll take you to the movies. How 'bout that? I'll take you to the park. We'll swing. We'll slide. Anything your heart desires. Stubbs? *(STUBBS releases his hold on COLONEL and grabs the sword with both hands. He steps one step back from the wheelchair and raises the sword in one quick and decisive movement, as though to decapitate the COLONEL, and then freezes in that posture. COLONEL stares straight ahead.)*

STUBBS *(through gas mask)*: GOD BLESS THE ENEMY!!!!!!! *(WHITE MAN, still sitting, facing right, starts singing.)*

WHITE MAN *(singing)*:
Sometimes I live in the country
Sometimes I live in the town
Sometimes I have a great notion
To jump into the river and drown

Irene, good night
Irene, good night
Good night, Irene
Good night, Irene
I'll see you in my dreams.

WHITE MAN *and* GLORY BEE *(singing)*:
Last Saturday night I got married
Me and my wife settled down
Now me and my wife are parted
I'm gonna take another stroll downtown

Irene, good night
Irene, good night
Good night, Irene
Good night, Irene
I'll see you in my dreams.©

WHITE MAN, GLORY BEE, *and* WHITE WOMAN *(singing)*:
    Stop ramblin', stop your gamblin'
    Stop stayin' out late at night
    Go home to your wife and your family
    Sit down by the fireside bright

    Irene, good night
    Irene, good night
    Good night, Irene
    Good night, Irene
    I'll see you in my dreams.

WHITE MAN, GLORY BEE, WHITE WOMAN, *and* COLONEL *(singing)*:
    I love Irene, God knows I do
    Love her 'til the seas run dry
    And if Irene turns her back on me
    I'm gonna take morphine and die

    Irene, good night
    Irene, good night
    Good night, Irene
    Good night, Irene
    I'll see you in my dreams.©

(The stage lights dim slowly to black, leaving STUBBS *and the* COLONEL *frozen.)*

END

far north

AN ALIVE FILMS PRODUCTION WITH NELSON ENTERTAINMENT
IN ASSOCIATION WITH CIRCLE JS PRODUCTIONS

A FILM BY SAM SHEPARD

FAR NORTH

Starring

JESSICA LANGE
CHARLES DURNING
TESS HARPER
DONALD MOFFAT
ANN WEDGEWORTH
PATRICIA ARQUETTE
NINA DRAXTEN

Written and Directed by
SAM SHEPARD

Produced by
CAROLYN PFEIFFER and MALCOLM HARDING

Editor
BILL YAHRAUS

Director of Photography
ROBBIE GREENBERG

Music Composed and Performed by
THE RED CLAY RAMBLERS

Production Designer
PETER JAMISON

Costume Designer
RITA SALAZAR

Associate Producer
JAMES KELLEY

Executive Producer
SHEP GORDON

EXTERIOR. NORTH WOODS—DAY.

CAMERA TRACKING FAST ACROSS the trunks of silver birch trees in dense forest. The movement is so fast the trees are blurred and barely recognizable. As titles roll, we hear: a large workhorse trotting hard on dirt and gravel; the horse snorting, blowing hard; a man's labored breathing; leather harness creaking; the sounds of buggy springs and rubber tires rolling fast.

(Titles end.)

CAMERA STILL TRACKING, pans onto the flaring nostrils and teeth of a big draft horse straining in his bridle at a breakaway trot. CAMERA PANS CLOSE along leather harness and lathered horseflesh to arrive close on an old man's burly, gnarled hands clutching the reins. Voice-over of the old man.

BERTRUM *(voice-over):* Mel! You meathead! Goddamnit, yer gonna kill us both! Whoa! You sonofabitch!

PAN ONTO BERTRUM, CLOSE: In his late sixties but built like an oak tree. He wears a pair of old brown coveralls, plaid shirt, work boots, and an old faded blue railroad cap with the Great Northern insignia on it (a mountain goat against the Rockies). He clutches the reins of a makeshift buckboard and tries desperately to control the runaway horse.

ANGLE ON BERTRUM'S BACK as the horse breaks into a gallop. The buckboard careens off the road, away from camera, heading straight for a ditch.

BERTRUM: Yer gonna be dogmeat when this is over! I'm sellin' you at the killer's price! Mel! Whoa!

Suddenly, the buckboard flips over completely when it hits the ditch, sending BERTRUM *headlong into a birch tree.*

Mel breaks loose from his harness, then stops, turns, and just stands there looking at the unconscious BERTRUM *and the overturned buckboard with the wheels still spinning. Vapor blasts from Mel's nostrils. A moment of total stillness, then the cry of a loon is heard in the distance.*

ANGLE ON ROAD.

CLOSE ON MEL'S EYE staring at the wreckage.

CUT TO:

INTERIOR. HOSPITAL HALLWAY—NEXT DAY.
CLOSE ON KATE staring into room through a window in the door. She is carrying a small plastic bag full of lemon drops. She is dressed in fashionable big-city clothes—dark skirt and jacket, white blouse, high heels. She is slightly rumpled from a recent airplane ride.

KATE'S POINT OF VIEW. She sees BERTRUM *splayed out in a hospital bed, IV bottles hanging around his head. He is apparently asleep, his breathing slow and labored. Behind him is a large picture window framing a view of Lake Superior with barges and tugboats inching their way across the background in the distance (mock-up).*

CLOSE ON KATE.

CLOSE ON KATE'S HANDS as she reaches into the bag of lemon drops without looking—a few fall to the floor. BACK ON KATE'S FACE, surprised. She looks down the hallway; a nurse is rolling a cart away. She fumbles to get all of the lemon drops back into the bag. She kicks the few she's missed and blows the dust off the ones in her hand.

REVERSE ANGLE—OVER BERTRUM ONTO KATE.
She tiptoes over to her father's bed and stares at his sleeping face,

bandaged and bruised. As she leans over to kiss his forehead he suddenly speaks to her, without opening his eyes. She pulls back.

BERTRUM: Pregnant?

KATE: Dad—

BERTRUM: You are, aren't ya? I can smell it. Pregnant women have this sweet smell they put off.

KATE: Could you at least open your eyes when you're talking to me? Makes me feel like we're in the same room together.

BERTRUM *(eyes shut)*: I don't need my eyes. I can smell it.

KATE: Well, we're off to a good start. Here, I brought you some lemon drops. Your favorite kind. You know. Those hard kind that stick to your teeth.

BERTRUM: When're ya gonna get married? Or is that still too old-fashioned for ya? Don't matter. Just try to make it a boy, if ya don't mind. Too damn many girls in the family as it is. Family's thick with women. Never used to be like that. Used to be men. All men.

KATE: Would you mind opening your eyes, Dad? I've been flying for hours and I'd like to see your eyes.

BERTRUM *pops his eyes open and stares at her.*

KATE *(continuing)*: Thanks.

BERTRUM *spots the bag of lemon drops. He snatches it out of her hand and digs one out, but can't manage to bring it up to his mouth from stiffness. He holds the lemon drop out to* KATE.

BERTRUM: Drop it in my mouth, would ya? I'm seized up.

BERTRUM *holds his mouth open like a bird.* KATE *drops it in.*

KATE: You had a wreck, huh?

BERTRUM: Bastard tried to kill me.

KATE: Mel?

BERTRUM: Yeah, Mel. Who else? He's had a grudge against me since the day he was foaled.

KATE: Well, it's no wonder, the way you treat him.

BERTRUM: I treat him like a horse! I don't pamper horses the way you women . . . . Whad'ya know about horses, anyway? Yer a big-city-girl now, aren't ya?

KATE: Aw, come on, Dad. Knock it off, will ya?

Awkward pause between them. BERTRUM *crunches down loudly on the lemon drop and grinds it between his teeth. He stares hard at* KATE. *She tries to force a smile.*

BERTRUM: Yer gonna have to shoot him for me. Ya know that, don't ya? Yer the only one I can trust to get it done.

KATE: I'm not gonna shoot your horse, Dad. I left my work. I dropped everything to come here and see you.

BERTRUM: That's what a daughter's supposed to do.

KATE: Yeah, well, I'm not shootin' your horse!

BERTRUM: Yer the only one mean enough! Now, you take that 30.06 in the cupboard—

KATE: Get Uncle Dane to do it or something. You honestly don't think that I'm gonna get a gun and—

BERTRUM: That drunk! Uncle Dane! Ha! He's across the hall right now, in detox. Couldn't hit a horse with an A-bomb.

KATE: Well, I'm not doing it! I didn't come all this way to shoot a horse. Dad, you just gotta relax now. It's not good for you to get so excited. I mean you're supposed to be taking it easy now. The horse can wait.

BERTRUM: It can't wait! He won't know what he's gettin' shot for if we wait!

KATE: Well, I'm not shooting him!

Pause, as KATE *just stares at him.* BERTRUM *cools down, settles back, disappointed in her. He gestures toward the bag of lemon drops. He points to his mouth.* KATE *takes one out of the bag and drops it into his mouth.*

CLOSE ON BERTRUM as he turns his head away from her and stares out the window, sucking on the lemon drop.

BERTRUM'S POINT OF VIEW of Lake Superior out the window. A huge cargo ship slowly creeps across the frame in the distance.

CLOSE ON BERTRUM.

BERTRUM *(staring out the window)*: You were my last hope. What I deserve for not havin' a son, I suppose.

CLOSE ON KATE. She makes a long exhale, tries to change the subject. We see a slight desperation come over her, as though trying to keep herself from sliding into old familiar emotional patterns with her father.

KATE: How's the rest of the family doing? Anybody else in the hospital?

BERTRUM: Not the ones who deserve it most.

KATE: Oh, like Mom, for instance?

BERTRUM: Nah, she's beyond the hospital.

KATE: Gramma, I suppose.

BERTRUM: There ya go. On the brink of a hundred. About to turn a round century this weekend. Can you believe that?

KATE: Oh, God. I forgot her birthday.

BERTRUM *(warming up to her)*: Katie—Katie—I haven't asked you for many favors in my time, now, have I?

KATE: Now, don't start up with that again.

BERTRUM: Well, somebody's got to avenge me! You're the only one left!

KATE: Avenge you? It's just a horse, for Christ's sake! It's a dumb old horse! He didn't know what he was doing!

BERTRUM: He knew, all right!

BERTRUM struggles to prop himself up on one elbow. He leans toward KATE and suddenly becomes very confidential.

BERTRUM: Here's what you wanna do. You draw an X. You take a piece of chalk and you draw a line from one ear to the opposite eye.

CLOSE ON KATE as BERTRUM continues. She sees she's getting nowhere with the old man. She sets the bag of lemon drops in his hand and starts to back out of the room as BERTRUM raves on.

BERTRUM: Then you do the same on the other side of his head. Now, where those two lines intersect, that's where you wanna put the bullet.

KATE *(backing out)*: I'll be back to see you tomorrow, Dad. You try and get some rest now.

KATE picks up her suitcase and heads out the door.

KATE'S POINT OF VIEW. CAMERA DOLLIES SLOWLY BACK, through the door, seeing BERTRUM receding in background as he rants on from the bed.

BERTRUM: You take the panel offa the kitchen cupboard. You know that secret panel? Rifle's in there.

KATE *(offscreen)*: Eat your lemon drops, Dad.

She blows him a kiss.

BERTRUM: Ammo's down in the basement. Make sure you git the right ammo! I don't want any slipups, now!

The door swings shut on him.

CUT TO:

INTERIOR. HOSPITAL CORRIDOR—SAME DAY.

Sudden collapse of overlapping sounds: television game shows, voices of patients, nurses, visitors, people eating, etc., as we dolly backward, in front of KATE, *down hallway.*

KATE'S POINT OF VIEW. Tracking past various rooms— sudden brief scenes appear in each room, then disappear into a blank pale green wall, then another scene appears, i.e., a woman, whose back is to camera, helps her crippled grandfather sit down in a chair—just a visual moment; then a bare leg appears, emerging from a sheet, in another room; in another room a man slowly lifts a spoon to his mouth, nothing more; a nurse takes a patient's pulse, etc. As camera keeps tracking in Kate's point of view, a racetrack announcer's voice on TV becomes dominant over the other sounds. The voice of the announcer rises with excitement as the horses close down the stretch.

CAMERA ARRIVES ON UNCLE DANE'S BACK. He is standing in one of the rooms watching the horse race on a TV mounted high on the wall. He is dressed in a hospital smock, hospital slippers, and a green baseball cap. He starts jumping up and down, cheering wildly as the winner crosses the finish line.

ANGLE ON KATE standing in corridor, watching UNCLE DANE, *whose back is to the door.*

KATE: Uncle Dane? Uncle Dane?

UNCLE DANE *whirls around to face her—still caught up in the delirium of his racing victory, slightly disoriented. He is a wiry man with a devilish fire in his eyes.*

UNCLE DANE: Manila! My Manila! Did you see that, honey? I knew he could do it! That was a horse race.

He grabs ahold of KATE *around the waist and does a little victory jig with her as he sings.* KATE *does her best to try to keep ahold of her suitcase.*

UNCLE DANE *(continuing; sings)*:
 Camptown races, five miles long,
 Doo-dah, doo-dah,
 Camptown ladies all day long,
 All the doo-dah day.

KATE: Uncle Dane, stop! Uncle Dane!

He stops and stares at her. KATE *straightens her clothes.*

KATE *(continuing)*: It's me. It's me. Katie.

His face breaks into a wide smile.

UNCLE DANE: Well. Of course it's you. Katie! Oh beautiful, beautiful Katie-Did.

He embraces her, pats her back softly.

UNCLE DANE: Well, who else could it be? You don't think I'd dance with any old gal that comes down the hallway, do ya?

KATE: What're you doing in here, Dane?

He stands back from her, slightly embarrassed, trying to make something up.

UNCLE DANE: Me? Aw, nothin'— Just a little checkup. You know. The usual routine. Heart. Lungs. Liver. Nothin' major. How 'bout yourself?

KATE: Oh, you know—Dad.

UNCLE DANE: Oh, yeah. Mr. Horseman. Serves him right. That horse shoulda killed him, way he treats animals. One a' these days a horse is gonna kill him. You wait and see. He's got it comin'.

KATE: Did you put yourself in here, Dane?

UNCLE DANE *(lying)*: Me? Nah—nah, not me. Friend a' mine. I just went along with it. Figured, what the hell? Few free meals. Chance to watch the big race. Now and then, you need a breather from the outside, don't ya think? Slacken the pace.

KATE: Yeah. I suppose.

UNCLE DANE: Well. You look fantastic, honey. How come you haven't been up to see us in so long?

KATE: Well, it's only been a month.

UNCLE DANE: Lot can happen in a month.

KATE: Yeah, looks that way.

UNCLE DANE: Don't let that big city steal you away from us, now.

Pause. KATE *smiles at him. Her face seems drawn and tired now.*

KATE: Dane? Have you ever shot a horse before?

REACTION ON UNCLE DANE.

UNCLE DANE: Only the losers.

CUT TO:

ANGLE ON KATE, SMILING.

CUT TO:

MEL TROTTING through the birch tree forest with a wide white X on his forehead.

CUT TO:

BIRCH TREE FOREST—WILDERNESS.

CUT TO:

HAYSTACKS.

CUT TO:

THE HOUSE.

CLOSE ON AN OLD BLACK-AND-WHITE PHOTO-
GRAPH of Kate's mother, Amy, holding a shaggy pony on a lead
with Kate and her sister, Rita, aged five and seven, sitting double
on the pony, bareback, all smiles. In the photo, Amy is a strikingly
beautiful young woman with an open smile and dressed up in the
high fashion of the forties, high heels, silk stockings, a dark suit, and
fancy hat—her best Sunday church clothes.

Voice-over of the women as their hands come into frame and touch
the photo.

RITA *(voice-over)*: My goodness, Katie, where did you find this?

KATE *(voice-over)*: Well, I found the negative up in Momma's old
suitcase. So I had it printed up. Thought maybe we could
give it to Gramma on her birthday.

CAMERA PULLS UP AND BACK to reveal the three
women in:

INTERIOR. AMY'S KITCHEN—EVENING.

RITA *and* AMY *are seated at a simple, Formica-topped kitchen table*
with the photo. RITA, *only a couple of years older than* KATE. AMY,
in her late sixties, with a fragile, dazed kind of beauty. KATE, *still*
dressed in the skirt and blouse from previous scene but now barefoot
and without the jacket, is standing on tiptoe on the kitchen counter
trying to pry loose a section of Sheetrock from the cupboard over the
sink with a butter knife. She works diligently at it as the scene
continues.

AMY: Oh, my goodness, will you look at that dress! I can't even
remember owning that dress. We'll have to get this framed.
Gramma'll just love it. Thanks so much, Katie.

KATE *finally pulls the panel free, revealing a large false space behind*
the cupboard, filled with Bertrum's rifles and shotguns.

RITA: Kate, what're you looking for, anyway?

KATE: Aah! Got it.

KATE *sets the panel by the sink and starts rummaging through the guns.*

AMY: What're you doing up there, honey?

KATE *(looking through guns)*: Dad wants me to shoot his horse.

Pause. RITA *and* AMY *exchange looks.*

RITA: What?

KATE: The horse he got in the wreck with.

RITA: Mel?

KATE: Yeah, Mel.

AMY: He just bought that horse, didn't he?

RITA: No, Momma, we've had Mel for a long, long time. Don't you remember Mel?

KATE: He wants me to shoot him.

RITA: Well, you're not gonna do it, are you? You're not gonna shoot Mel?

KATE: I don't know. I've never shot anything before in my life. I don't even know how to shoot a gun.

RITA: Well, you can't shoot Mel! That's murder! It's not the poor horse's fault.

AMY: Of course it isn't.

RITA: I'm surprised you'd even consider this, Kate.

KATE *pulls a shotgun out of the hiding place and examines it.*

KATE: Surprised me, too. He told me I had to avenge him.

AMY: Oh, my goodness! The cookies!

AMY *rushes to the stove and takes out a tray full of fresh cookies and sets them on top of the stove.*

KATE *sticks the shotgun back and searches for another gun.*

RITA: Kate, you're not serious about this, arc you? I mean, you know how he is. He's always wantin' to shoot somethin'. As soon as somethin' goes wrong, he wants to shoot it. Doesn't mean it.

AMY: He's shot all our dogs.

RITA: No, Momma.

KATE *pulls down a deer rifle and shows it to* RITA.

KATE: Is this a 30.06?

RITA: I'm not tellin' you if it's a 30.06! Mel used to be my horse, don't forget! I learned to ride on Mel.

KATE *climbs off the counter, mounts the rifle to her shoulder, and aims it across the room.* RITA *immediately jumps up from the table and backs away fast.*

RITA *(continuing)*: Don't point that thing in the house! It could be loaded! Are you crazy?!

AMY *(from the stove)*: Katie, don't play with guns in the house. We don't do that in the house.

KATE: All right. Take it easy.

KATE *lowers rifle and sits. She puts the rifle across her lap.* RITA *moves to* KATE *and takes the rifle.*

RITA: Here, let me see this. He's always leaving loaded guns around. You shouldn't take a chance with it.

RITA *cracks the lever several times to make sure it's empty. It's obvious she's had some experience with weapons.*

KATE: Now, what's the trick, anyway? I mean, you know, say somebody wanted to shoot something with it?

RITA: You mean, like a horse?

RITA *hands the rifle back to* KATE, *confident that it's empty.* KATE *again mounts the rifle to her shoulder and aims it at the TV set in the living room.*

KATE *(sighting down barrel)*: How do you aim it?

RITA: You see that bead up at the end of the barrel?

KATE'S POINT OF VIEW—sighting down barrel of rifle with the TV in the distance.

BACK TO SCENE.

KATE: Yeah.

RITA: You line that up so it's right in the center of the back sight. That little "V" thing there.

KATE: Yeah, right.

The rifle suddenly explodes with a live cartridge, blowing a huge smoking hole right through the TV set. RITA *screams.*

CUT TO:

EXTERIOR. FIELD—DAY.

Shrill, haunting sound of a loon calling from a distant lake, as CAMERA TRACKS FAST, chasing Bertrum's horse, Mel, as he gallops full tilt across an open field, as though in response to the rifle shot.

CUT TO:

INTERIOR. HOSPITAL ROOM—SAME NIGHT.

BERTRUM *sits up fast in bed, out of a dead sleep, shaking off a nightmare. The room is in darkness except for the distant glow of lights from ships anchored in the lake and a dim light from the hallway. His door is open. He stares straight at the open doorway.* UNCLE DANE *is standing there, silhouetted in the doorway, staring back at* BERTRUM. *Just a brief moment, then* UNCLE DANE *ducks down the hallway and disappears.*

BERTRUM: Dane? That you?

BERTRUM stares at the empty doorway. A mournful wail from a foghorn is heard from the lake. BERTRUM turns toward the window and stares out. Sounds of teenagers, laughing and giggling over.

CUT TO:

EXTERIOR. CAR—SAME NIGHT.

A car is parked in front of Amy and Bertrum's house with a TEENAGE BOY slouched down behind the wheel, trying to stay hidden from view of the house.

In the backseat, Rita's daughter, JILLY, is necking passionately with ANOTHER BOY. They roll off the backseat onto the floor, giggling hysterically and very drunk.

BOY IN FRONT SEAT: Come on, goddamnit! It's my turn, Mike!

JILLY *(on floor in back)*: I don't give turns! I just give head!

JILLY and MIKE laugh wildly as the BOY in front starts climbing over the seat into the back. Sounds of bottles and beer cans crashing as he goes.

CUT TO:

INTERIOR. HOUSE—SAME NIGHT.

RITA and KATE are kneeling on the sofa in the living room, peering out at the car through the curtains. The blasted TV is in the background.

KATE: You've gotta go out there.

RITA: I'm not goin' out there! Are you crazy? I'm not making a fool of myself in front of a bunch of teenage assholes!

KATE: It's your own daughter, Rita!

RITA: I'll wait 'til she gets in the house, if you don't mind.

KATE *(getting up)*: Then I'm gonna go.

RITA: No! Katie, you can't go out there!

KATE: She could be getting raped out there, Rita!

RITA: She's not getting raped, believe me. *They're* getting raped.

KATE: That's a horrible thing to say.

   KATE *heads for the door, picking up the rifle off the kitchen table as she goes.*

RITA: You can't go out there! Katie! Put that gun back! You don't know how to use a gun. You've proved that already!

KATE *exits house.*

CUT TO:

EXTERIOR. CAR—TEENAGERS' POINT OF VIEW OF KATE—SAME NIGHT.

As front door slams and they see KATE *charging off the front porch with the rifle leveled at the car.*

MEDIUM DOLLY SHOT ON KATE, PULLING BACK WITH HER as she heads toward car.

KATE *(aiming rifle)*: Jilly! You come outta there! You get outta there right now!

REVERSE—KATE'S POINT OF VIEW—TRACKING TOWARD CAR. The headlights of the car pop on as the ignition turns over. The BOYS *can be seen scrambling wildly, pulling their pants up, trying to get the car in gear.*

ANGLE ON KATE, still moving.

KATE: Jilly, if you don't get outta that car right now, I'm gonna shoot the tires off it! You hear me?!

ANGLE ON CAR. The car backs up in fits and spurts, cutting a wide U-turn through the gravel driveway. A back door pops open and JILLY *spills out onto the ground as the car spits gravel and careens off down the road.*

KATE *pursues the car for a short distance, brandishing the rifle, then stops and returns to* JILLY, *who is picking herself up off the ground, adjusting her clothes, and rubbing her knee.*

JILLY *teeters drunkenly and almost falls back down as* KATE *comes up to her and smiles warmly.*

KATE: Well, I wondered what you did for recreation up here.

JILLY: Aunt Kate? What're you doin' here?

KATE *(smiling)*: I just came to shoot a horse.

REACTION ON JILLY.

CUT TO:

INTERIOR. HOSPITAL ROOM—LATER SAME NIGHT.

UNCLE DANE *is crawling, marine style, across the floor of Bertrum's room with a bottle of black Navy Rum tucked under his arm. He is trying to be as quiet and stealthy as possible.* BERTRUM *is sound asleep. Vague, broken sounds of TV and an occasional moan from a patient down the hallway.* BERTRUM *sleeps on as* UNCLE DANE *reaches the foot of his bed. He grabs* BERTRUM *by the foot and shakes it, but* BERTRUM *remains asleep.*

UNCLE DANE *(heavy whisper)*: Bertrum! I brought you some medicine. A hundred-ten proof! It'll open yer plumbing for ya. Guaranteed.

He shakes BERTRUM's *foot again.*

UNCLE DANE *(continuing)*: Bertrum!

BERTRUM *jerks awake, trying to sit up, thrashing with his arms and kicking at the foot of the bed as if he's seen a snake. He speaks in a delirium until he realizes where he is.*

BERTRUM: Aaaah!! Put the halter on him! Get that halter on him!

UNCLE DANE: Shhhh! It's me! Dane. Don't make all that noise. You'll send everybody in here.

BERTRUM: Where's Kate? Did she get him?

UNCLE DANE *sneaks around the bed and sits besides* BERTRUM, *secretly showing him the bottle of rum.*

UNCLE DANE: Look what I got ya.

BERTRUM: What're you doin' in here? Get offa this bed, ya meathead!

BERTRUM *kicks* UNCLE DANE *off the bed.*

UNCLE DANE: I thought you might like to celebrate my winnings with me. I won today, in case ya didn't know.

UNCLE DANE *cracks the bottle open with a grin.*

BERTRUM: You won what? Where'd you get that bottle, anyway?

UNCLE DANE: I've got my connections.

UNCLE DANE *grins at* BERTRUM *and takes a long pull on the bottle.*

CUT TO:

INTERIOR. AMY'S HOUSE—NIGHT.

Sounds of JILLY *vomiting violently and banging on the walls of the bathroom as* CAMERA IS CLOSE ON KATE'S HANDS *cracking raw eggs into a glass and then pouring white vinegar into it.*

PULL BACK *to see* KATE *in kitchen, making her concoction for Jilly while* RITA *paces furiously back and forth, through the living room, blaring out a lecture to the unseen* JILLY *who keeps moaning from the bathroom.*

RITA: No more dates for six weeks! Six whole weeks! You got that?

JILLY *moans.*

RITA *(continuing)*: No phone calls! No letters! I'm cuttin' you off, sister!

KATE *has finished mixing up the eggs and vinegar potion and moves through the living room with the glass to offer it to* JILLY. *She passes* RITA.

KATE: Keep it down, you guys. You're gonna wake up Momma.

RITA *(to* JILLY*)*: If a boy so much as calls this house, I'm tellin' him you moved! Far away to another country, where they don't speak English!

KATE *knocks softly on bathroom door, then opens it.* JILLY *comes crawling out on her hands and knees, slapping the floor with her hands and moaning. She keeps moving around the living room floor in circles on all fours as* KATE *follows her closely with the glass of raw eggs, trying to get her to drink it.* RITA *keeps pacing and raving.*

KATE *(following* JILLY *with glass)*: Jilly? Jilly, stand up now and drink this. It'll settle your stomach.

JILLY *keeps crawling, moaning, and slapping the floor as* KATE *follows her.*

RITA: You think it's lonely now? You're gonna wish you'd never been born in the Great North Woods.

KATE: Oh, shut up, Rita! She needs some help now. Will you stop preaching at her? Jilly, stand up and drink this. Now.

JILLY *keeps crawling and moaning.*

RITA: Get up off the floor, girl!!

AMY *wanders into the kitchen, adjusting her bathrobe and bleary-eyed from being woken.*

AMY: Is Bertrum home?

RITA: No, Momma. We've got everything under control here. You go back to bed now.

AMY *(half awake)*: Oh. There was so much noise, I thought he might've come home.

KATE: Come on, Jilly, stand up and drink this now! Come on!!

JILLY: I'm gonna be sick.

AMY *stares at* JILLY *crawling in circles, not quite comprehending.*

AMY: Did she lose something on the floor?

RITA: No, Momma. She's just a little bit sick. Please go on back to bed now.

AMY: Oh, Jilly. She's the young one. They're always sick.

AMY *turns and heads back to bed. CAMERA MOVES WITH HER, on her back.*

ANGLE ON KATE.

CUT TO:

INTERIOR. HOSPITAL ROOM—SAME NIGHT.

BERTRUM *and* UNCLE DANE, *sitting side by side on the bed, backs to camera, staring out the window at the lights of Lake Superior, passing the bottle of rum between them. They are getting well oiled by now.*

BERTRUM *(drunk)*: I never thought there'd come a time, Dane, when I'd stop missing women. I just don't miss 'em anymore. Now, why is that?

UNCLE DANE *(drunker)*: Well, you got other things on yer mind, Bertrum.

BERTRUM: That's right. Other things.

UNCLE DANE: More important. You got some plans now, don't ya?

BERTRUM: Plans— Yeah. I got some plans. But— There was a time when the only thing I ever had on my mind was Amy. She was the only thing. Can you believe that?

*CAMERA IS SLOWLY PIVOTING, throughout this dia-
logue, around them in 180 degrees until, by the end, it arrives full
front in a two-shot.*

UNCLE DANE: That was a while back, wasn't it?

BERTRUM: While back. On the railroad. Nothin' much to do on
the railroad but think about women. *(Pause.)* Now, look at
these gals a' mine. These two daughters. Neither one of
'em's got a man. They got kids, all right. They get knocked
up but they got no man.

UNCLE DANE: Where's the man?

BERTRUM: Well, that's what I'd like to know. Where in the hell
is the goddamn man? Used to be, when you got a girl in
trouble, that was it. You got married. That was all she wrote.

UNCLE DANE: That's right. That was pretty much the end of the
line, in those days.

BERTRUM: You didn't run off and ditch her—leave her to her
own devices. Aw, who the hell knows what they do on their
own these days. They go off away to the city, come back
pregnant, and they got no goddamn man.

UNCLE DANE: Well, they'll find one, Bertrum. Don't you worry.
They'll get a man. Those are good-lookin' gals you got.

BERTRUM: Where? Where they gonna find one? Not up here,
that's for sure. No men left up here. No man in his right
mind's gonna stay up here in this Christless country. 'Cept
us. And there's not a whole lot left of us.

UNCLE DANE: Well, we were born here. This is where we were
born and raised, Bertrum.

Pause. BERTRUM *just stares at him a second, then explodes.*

BERTRUM: You don't have to tell me where I was born and
raised! I know damn well where I was born and raised!

UNCLE DANE: I was just sayin'—that's the reason we're here.

BERTRUM: What's the reason?

UNCLE DANE: The reason we never left is 'cause we were born here.

Pause. BERTRUM *stares at him a second. Shakes his head in disbelief.*

BERTRUM: Oh, you are a piss-poor excuse for a relative. You know that?

BERTRUM *snatches the bottle away from* UNCLE DANE *and takes a long hard chug on it.*

INTERIOR. BATHROOM.

JILLY *is hugging the toilet bowl, moaning.*

INTERIOR. AMY'S HOUSE.

KATE *and* RITA, *in their bathrobes, talking to each other over the blown-out TV set.*

RITA: I don't wanna end up raising my daughter in the house I grew up in.

KATE: Well, I can think of worse things.

RITA: Like what?

KATE: Well, like, I don't know, not having a place to come back to. Look, you know when I first left here, there wasn't a thing I had in my mind except to get as far away from this place as I possibly could. I mean, far. I didn't care if I never saw another birch tree as long as I lived.

RITA: So why'd you come back, then?

KATE: Dad. Dad's in the hospital, in case you forgot.

KATE *and* RITA *bend down and grab opposite ends of the TV and lift it slowly, as they continue their conversation. They start carrying the TV slowly through the house toward the back door, struggling with the weight of it. Camera dollies with them as the dialogue continues:*

RITA: I know Dad's in the hospital. Christ, Kate.

KATE: No, I don't know, it's more than that. I guess it's family, you know. Ever since you called me about his accident, I've been feeling this thing.

RITA: What thing?

KATE: Like time is running out or something. Like this might be my last chance with him.

They reach the back door, open it, and go out into a small wooden porch with a railing that drops steeply down into a little ditch. Bright moonlight. Sounds of frogs and night bugs.

RITA: Last chance for what?

KATE: Just to do something for him.

RITA: Well, you know him. Whatever it is, he won't be satisfied.

KATE: Maybe. No harm in trying.

They hoist the TV up on the guardrail of the porch and balance it there.

RITA: Kate, if you kill that horse, I'm never gonna speak to you again in my whole life.

KATE *(smiling)*: He told me I was the only one mean enough.

KATE gives the TV a shove and it goes end over end, crashing into the gorge below with a white explosion.

CUT TO:

INTERIOR. HOSPITAL ROOM—SAME NIGHT.

BERTRUM *is now rolling drunk and ranting at the world in general. He crashes around the room like a rabid bear.* UNCLE DANE *is in*

even worse shape, but all he can do is switch the channels on the TV
aimlessly, half listening to BERTRUM'*s tirade.*

BERTRUM: The main issue! The main issue of the world at large
is one thing and one thing only. And you wanna know what
that one thing is?

UNCLE DANE: There isn't any main issue. There never has been
a main issue. Just keep it down, Bertrum. You're supposed
to stay in bed now.

BERTRUM: Injustice! That's the main issue! And what's the flip
side of injustice? Justice! That's it in a nutshell. Justice and
Injustice. That's the two main issues of the world today.

UNCLE DANE: I thought there was only one main issue.

ANGLE ON TV SCREEN as DANE *flips through the channels.*

BACK TO BERTRUM AND DANE in the room.

BERTRUM: Now, in a case like government—big government—
United Nations kin'a stuff. You think they give a rat's
diddly-ass about a lone, single citizen like myself, for instance? Up here in the frontier—locked away from the
world in the far north of America? A man who's fought in
the trenches of Italy; in the slime of Korea; who broke his
back on the railroad tracks of Lake Erie! Do you think they
give one diddly-poop about his own personal sense of Justice? Hey, not on your long johns.

BERTRUM *takes a rest. He stares out the window at the lights.*
Takes a swig from the bottle.

BERTRUM *(continuing; to himself)*: And that's exactly the reason
why I'm gonna shoot that horse in the head. That's exactly
the reason, right there.

CUT TO:

CLOSE ON MEL'S HEAD surrounded by blackness, as in a
vision. There are two white chalk lines drawn on his black face,

exactly as Bertrum described to Kate—one from each ear to the opposite eye, forming a large X in the center of his face. His eyes are wild and fearful. A loud gunshot is heard on the cut.

CUT TO:

INTERIOR. AMY'S HOUSE—BEDROOM—EARLY MORNING.

KATE *sits up fast in bed, shaking off the vision. Her eyes pop open. She's not sure where she is.*

A QUICK SERIES OF IMAGES of what she sees: A red squirrel out the window, skittering along a tree branch. A photo of Bertrum in army uniform with Amy in a wedding gown, on top of a bureau.

A quick flash of New York City street, throbbing with thousands of people. KATE*'s point of view of the bedroom door.*

CLOSE ON KATE realizing where she is. She hears the sounds of JILLY *moaning with a hangover. The sounds of eggs frying in a skillet.*

CUT TO:

CLOSE ON TWO SUNNY-SIDE-UP EGGS crackling in a pan in Amy's kitchen. Voice-overs of RITA *and* AMY *with* JILLY*'s moans heard in the background.*

RITA *(offscreen):* Jilly, you don't stop that moanin', you can go out in the barn.

ANGLE ON KITCHEN—EARLY MORNING.

RITA *is standing, on tiptoe, up on the counter, putting the secret panel back together. The deer rifle lies on the counter below her.* AMY *is at the stove, fixing a huge breakfast—much more than the four of them can actually eat. The table is set for four with stacks of steaming pancakes, toast, sausage, coffee, biscuits—the whole works.* AMY *has gone overboard, as though she's been cooking for all her relatives and ancestors included.*

AMY: Maybe you oughta take her some juice, honey.

RITA: Let her suffer. It's the only way she'll learn.

AMY: Well, you don't wanna let her get dehydrated. It's the difference between suffering and torture.

RITA: I think I'm gonna have to hide this gun.

AMY: Oh, now, honey, Katie's not actually gonna do anything. She could no more shoot a horse than a fly. You know how Kate is. She just talks. Just like her father.

> RITA *climbs down from counter with the rifle.*

RITA: Well, she's got this crazy idea in her head that she owes Dad something and I don't trust it.

AMY: Well, they've always had a strange relationship. It'll pass. Don't you worry.

RITA *(with rifle)*: This thing's already done enough damage as it is. I'm gonna put it out in the barn.

AMY: Well, wait 'til after breakfast, honey. It's almost ready now.

RITA: I wanna get it out of here before she gets up.

> RITA *moves with rifle, toward front door.*

AMY: Rita, everything's going to get cold!

RITA: Mom, are you sure you made enough stuff, huh?

> RITA *passes Jilly's bedroom on the way to door.* JILLY *moans loudly.*

RITA *(continuing)*: Pipe down in there, sister! It's your own fault you've got a headache!

> RITA *exits out front door.*

QUICK CUT TO:

INTERIOR. JILLY'S BATHROOM—SAME TIME.

> JILLY, *looking very pale and drawn, slams her fists into the walls in response to her mother.*

CUT BACK TO:

AMY, left alone in kitchen, facing an empty table filled with food.

AMY *(to herself)*: Oh, well. Carry on as though you're still in the land of the living.

She turns and goes back to the stove, as though resigned to continue with her duties, no matter what.

AMY *(continuing)*: That was the thing. That was always the thing with Mother. Bless her heart. Only difference today is a notable lack of menfolk. There used to always be men. Always.

As she turns from the stove to carry more food to the table, suddenly the small Formica table is transformed into a long plank farm table, with farmhands and the men of her past. BERTRUM is there, at the head, much younger, in grimy overalls and work shirt. Big, burly uncles and cousins, all different ages. All men. They are digging into their breakfasts and ignore AMY's presence. Loud conversation, boisterous laughter, pipe smoke, and steaming coffee. AMY continues in the scene as though this were strictly her memory. She remains in the present, dressed the same. She sets more food down in front of them and circles the table with a pot of coffee, reaching over and between them to fill their cups. She keeps talking to herself through all this.

AMY *(as she circles table)*: A giant big ring of men. Elbows. Big beefy legs and knees. Had to serve them above their heads. Over and above with the gravy. You could never squeeze between. They wouldn't let you get between them and their food. No room at all. Not that we minded. Who could stand to eat beside them anyway.

AMY returns to the stove with the coffeepot. She sets the pot down.

As AMY passes an alcove doorway, KATE appears, brushing her teeth, wearing a bathrobe. She just stands there and watches her mother, listening casually to her. She's become used to Amy's running monologues. AMY *pays no attention to* KATE's *presence. It's as though she's in a world of her own.*

AMY *(continuing; to herself)*: Kinda miss it, though. Just the smell of them. Miss that sometimes. *(Pause.)* I don't know whatever became of them. What became of them, Kate? Where'd they all go?

QUICK ANGLE ON FORMICA TABLE with all the food steaming and no men now.

BACK TO THE PRESENT.

ON KATE. She moves across kitchen to sink and finishes brushing her teeth.

KATE: They're in the hospital, Momma.

AMY *turns and stares at the empty table with four plates set.*

AMY *(continuing)*: They used to be at the table.

AMY *stares at* KATE, *brushing her teeth.*

AMY *(continuing)*: Where's your man, Kate? Don't you have a man?

KATE, *caught off-guard by the question, rinses her mouth, grabs a dishtowel.*

KATE: Sure. He's in the city, Momma. Business. You know, I had to come here so fast because of Dad.

AMY: Have I ever met him?

KATE: I—uh—I don't think so.

AMY: Do you think I ever will?

KATE *moves to the table, trying to avoid the trend in the conversation.*

KATE: Sure— Boy, look at this breakfast. You really outdid yourself, Mom. Are we having company or something?

AMY: Well, you can take whatever's left over to the hospital when you visit. Some sausage and biscuits. The men'll like that.

KATE *sits at the table, surveying the spread. She smiles at her mother's efforts. Pours herself a cup of coffee.* AMY *sits at the opposite side of the table.* KATE *studies her face with affection.*

KATE: Hey, Momma, why don't you come back to the city with me, huh?

AMY: What city?!

KATE: New York.

AMY *(laughs)*: Oh, no! No, I could never go to the city.

KATE: Oh, come on. Just for a visit. It would do you good to get out of this place.

AMY *(embarrassed)*: What would I do in the city?

KATE: Well, there's lots of stuff we could do. I mean we could go to concerts and museums, operas—there are lots of things to do.

AMY *(giggles)*: Operas?

KATE: Yeah. You've never been to an opera, have you?

AMY: Well, they're in a foreign language, aren't they?

KATE: Yeah—

AMY: No, I could never leave Bertrum and Momma here alone.

KATE: Why not?

AMY: They need me.

KATE: Yeah, but Momma, you gotta do something for yourself once in a while. I mean, look. Dad's a full-grown man, he can take care of himself.

AMY: He's in the hospital.

JILLY *moans in the background.* KATE *turns toward the sound.*

KATE: Oh, God. I'll bet she's got a head as big as a tire today, huh?

AMY: Rita wouldn't even take her in some juice. I don't understand that. She must be so dehydrated by now.

JILLY *moans.*

KATE: Where is Rita?

AMY: Oh, she took that gun out to the barn. Afraid you were going to kill something with it.

KATE *stands fast.*

KATE: She took the gun to the barn?

AMY: Now, don't *you* leave the table too. Katie!

KATE: She never could mind her own damn business!

KATE *leaves for the barn. Heads for the front door.*

AMY: Katie! You come back here and eat your breakfast! ˙

CUT TO:

INTERIOR. JILLY'S BATHROOM—SAME MORNING.

Close on Jilly, her head in the sink with water running over it. She raises her head, water pouring down her face, staring out the window toward the barn.

STILL IN POINT OF VIEW. As KATE *approaches barn,* RITA *comes exploding out of it, riding Mel bareback at a full gallop, heading straight toward* KATE. *All in long shot.*

ANGLE ON JILLY FULL FRONT, seeing her mother and Mel.

BACK TO JILLY'S POINT OF VIEW—WIDE. She sees KATE *grab* RITA *by the foot and drag her to the ground as Mel goes galloping by.*

BACK TO JILLY— CLOSE. She clutches her head, eyes wide, as though believing this must be some hallucination.

MEDIUM ON MEL as he comes charging straight toward Jilly's bathroom window, looking as if he's going to crash right through it.

ON JILLY. She screams and climbs the toilet seat, trying to escape the onslaught.

ON MEL as he ducks off at the last second and crashes off toward the woods.

ON JILLY. She climbs onto the toilet—screams.

EXTERIOR. BARNYARD—SAME TIME.

RITA *is lying on the ground with* KATE *standing over her. Reminiscent of an old western.*

RITA *(struggling to her feet)*: Are you crazy? You coulda killed us both!

KATE: Where's the gun, Rita?

CLOSE ON AMY as she gently opens Jilly's bedroom door and peeks her head in.

AMY *(sweet)*: Breakfast is served!

CLOSE ON JILLY standing on top of toilet seat, eyes terrified, squeezing her head between her hands.

JILLY *(screams)*: Get me out of Minnesota!

CUT TO:

MEL as he runs through the woods with his bridle and reins flapping loose.

CUT TO:

AN EAGLE coasting against the blue of the trees.

CUT TO:

CLOSE ON GRAMMA'S HANDS, crossed, on her lap, on a crocheted blanket.

CUT TO:

EXTERIOR. NEIGHBORHOOD OF SMALL SUB-URB—CLOSE ON GRAMMA'S HANDS CROSSED OVER.

One hundred years old and still full of spunk. She is bundled up in blankets and sweaters, being pushed in her wheelchair by AMY *down a broken, frost-heaved sidewalk in a neighborhood straight out of the thirties. There are no cars and no people in the background. The wheelchair bumps along violently.*

CAMERA BEGINS ON GRAMMA'S HANDS, crossed in her lap, then slowly pulls back to see GRAMMA *herself, continues to pull back, revealing* AMY, *then holds them both as it dollies backward to the end of the scene.*

GRAMMA: Oh, this is terrible! This is the worst! Where's my Katie? Is my Katie here? She wouldn't allow this to happen to me. She wouldn't allow it.

AMY: She's at the hospital, Momma. With Dad.

GRAMMA: She's not injured, is she?

AMY: No, Momma. Dad's injured.

GRAMMA: He was born injured.

AMY: She's going to be here for your birthday, Momma.

GRAMMA: Birthday? I'm not having a birthday, am I?

AMY: This Sunday, Momma. This Sunday's your birthday.

GRAMMA: Sunday? I can't have a birthday on the Sabbath. Check the calendar. That's not right. Somebody's made a mistake about that.

AMY: No, this Sunday's your birthday, Momma.

GRAMMA: That couldn't be right. Is Rita here?

AMY: She's at the house.

GRAMMA: Well, you ask Rita or Dane. They'll tell you. It's never been on a Sunday before. That's not right. How could it fall on a Sunday? There's church. No one will come.

AMY: We're having a big party planned for you.

GRAMMA: No one will be there. You'll see. No one's gonna miss church to go to a party. Oh, this is just terrible. Can't we go back inside?

AMY: You need the sun, Momma. It's good for you.

GRAMMA: It's torture. This family loves to torture me. Why is that? Where are my girls?

INTERIOR. LIVING ROOM—AMY'S HOUSE— SAME DAY.

RITA is sprawled out on the sofa on her back with pillows propped under her and a wet washrag on her forehead. JILLY sits beside her, trying to offer her a cup of tea. RITA moans and squirms, but there's more a sense that she's been deeply insulted by Kate than injured.

JILLY: Don't ya think I oughta call the doctor, Mom? I mean, maybe you've really messed up your back.

RITA: No! No doctors! I hate doctors!

JILLY: You want some tea?

RITA: Jilly—listen to me. *(Sudden secrecy.)* We've got to save Mel. You and me.

JILLY: Mel. Whatsa matter with Mel? He seems fine to me.

RITA leans toward JILLY. Very intense, in a low whisper.

RITA: Kate is trying to kill him!

CLOSE ON JILLY dumbfounded, trying to comprehend through her hangover.

JILLY: You want an Alka-Seltzer, maybe?

RITA: Jilly! You're not listenin' to me!

JILLY: I am, Mom. Aunt Katie's trying to kill Mel. That's what you said, right?

RITA: We've got to get Mel outta here, fast. Before she gets back.

JILLY: Mom, why would Aunt Katie wanna kill Mel? That's crazy.

RITA: *She's* crazy! That's why. She is. I mean, look at this. Look at what she did to me! If she can do something like this to her sister, then what's she going to do to a horse?

JILLY: I don't know.

RITA: Jilly, I can't let anything happen to Mel. He's part of the family.

JILLY: I know, Mom, but—I know.

RITA: Listen. You go out there to the barn and get a bucket. Put some grain in it and shake it. He always comes when he hears that bucket.

JILLY: He's way out in the woods, Mom. He's halfway to Duluth by now.

RITA: He'll hear you. He always comes when he hears that bucket.

JILLY: I'm not feelin' so hot. I gotta go out in the woods and catch a horse! I can't believe this! Come on.

RITA: All right, then I'll do it myself.

RITA tries to haul herself up out of the sofa. She winces with back pain. JILLY pushes her back down and stands.

JILLY: Fine. Then fine. I'm going, okay? Just sit still. Jesus! I thought this was supposed to be a family.

CUT TO:

EXTERIOR. MEL IN THE WOODS with the white X mark on his head.

CUT TO:

INTERIOR. BERTRUM'S HOSPITAL ROOM—SAME DAY.

Close on BERTRUM *unconscious in bed, looking very pale. He is hooked up to oxygen. His eyes are closed and his breathing is slow and labored.*

Voice-over of NURSE, *speaking to* KATE *in background.*

NURSE *(voice-over)*: He collapsed earlier this morning. We have no idea how he could've gotten ahold of liquor, but there was a very high alcohol content in his blood.

CLOSE ON KATE'S HAND taking BERTRUM's. *She squeezes. He squeezes back.*

CLOSE ON KATE.

KATE: Dad? I brought you some sausage and biscuits. Momma made a huge breakfast. You shoulda seen it. Looked just like Thanksgiving. I don't know what she was thinking about.

CLOSE ON BERTRUM. He smiles and squeezes her hand. His eyes stay closed.

ANGLE ON KATE.

KATE: You can hear me, right? Can you hear me, Dad?

BERTRUM *smiles again and squeezes her hand.*

KATE *(continuing)*: What'd you have to go and do this for? You were getting so much better. They were gonna let you out in a couple of days. *(Pause; she stares at him.)* It was Uncle Dane, wasn't it. Dane had a bottle.

Pause. She stares at her father's face, watching him breathe. She looks at the maze of machinery he's hooked up to. She listens to his breathing. She stares out the window.

KATE'S POINT OF VIEW—LAKE SUPERIOR.

ANGLE ON KATE.

KATE: Dad? I gotta tell you something. Can you hear me? It's about Mel.

ON BERTRUM. A flicker of recognition passes across him at the mention of his horse's name.

KATE: Something happened at home. I mean . . . *(She takes a breath.)* . . . Mel ran away.

BERTRUM *suddenly starts getting upset. He squeezes hard on* KATE's *hand. A rumbling sound comes from his throat. His jaw tenses.*

KATE *(continuing)*: Now, don't get upset. I'll find him for you. It'll be all right. Don't worry about it. I'll get him back. He just ran off into the woods a little ways. *(Pause.)* Rita turned him loose.

BERTRUM *responds again, grinding his teeth, clenching his fist and pulling at the sheet.*

KATE *(continuing)*: She's real attached to him, I guess. I mean, I didn't realize how much Mel meant to her. You can't really blame her, though. I mean, she used to ride him all the time.

BERTRUM *slams the bed with his fist.*

KATE *(continuing)*: I'll find him, Dad. Don't worry about it. The thing is— Look, Dad— The thing is, I just don't know if I can shoot him. I just don't think I can do that.

BERTRUM *jerks his hand away from* KATE's. *She tries to grab ahold of it again, but he pulls it away and turns his head away from her.* KATE *just stands there, holding the basket full of biscuits and sausage, on the verge of tears.*

KATE *(continuing)*: I'd like to do something for you. I really would, but I just don't think I can do that. Isn't there something else you could ask me to do? I'll do anything you want, huh?

BERTRUM *rejects her.*

BERTRUM *jerks his head back toward her. His eyes open. His face reddens. He seems on the verge of a temper tantrum, like he's about to explode. He starts to shake and tremble with rage.* KATE *sets the basket of food down and does her best to calm him. She puts her hands on his shoulders.*

KATE *(continuing)*: Now, listen. Don't get excited. Come on—come on. Don't sit up. You're not supposed to get excited. Dad! It's all right.

She tries to push him back down in the bed as he struggles.

KATE *(continuing)*: All right—Dad. Listen. Are you listening to me? I'll do it. I'll shoot the horse. All right.

Pause. BERTRUM *settles back. Relaxes.*

KATE *(continuing)*: I'll do it just like you said. Is that what you want?

BERTRUM *smiles. He takes her hand again and squeezes.*

KATE *(continuing)*: I'll take him out in the woods and tie him to a tree and shoot him. All right?

BERTRUM *nods and smiles. His eyes close again and he falls asleep. His hand grows limp in* KATE's.

KATE *(continuing)*: And then, maybe—maybe we can be friends.

She tucks BERTRUM's *hand under the sheet and kisses him on the forehead. She sets the basket of food on his night table. She looks at him as he sleeps and breathes through the machine. She runs her hand through his hair gently.*

CUT TO:

EXTERIOR. WOODS BEHIND THE BARN—SAME AFTERNOON.

JILLY *is moving very slowly through the trees, shaking a feed bucket and clucking for Mel. She hides a halter and lead rope behind her back to Mel won't notice her intentions. Mel is even deeper in the woods, with his neck arched and his ears cocked toward* JILLY. *He stares at her as she tries to coax him to come to her with the bucket.*

JILLY: Mel, come on. Come on, you little knucklehead. Look what I brought you. Nobody's gonna hurt you. You don't have to be afraid. Look—some oats. Come and smell these good old oats, Mel. These are some really good old oats. See?

She takes a handful of oats out of the bucket and tosses them in her mouth. She chews them a few times, then spits them out. Mel keeps a close eye on her behavior.

JILLY *(continuing)*: I can't believe I'm doing this.

JILLY *digs her hands into the oats and offers some out to Mel. Mel moves in a little closer to her, sniffing for the oats, but still wary.*

JILLY *(continuing)*: Atsa good boy. You don't have to be afraid. Nobody's gonna hurt you. Granpa's not around. You put him in the hospital. He isn't anywhere near here, Mel. Just you and me, and I'm not gonna hurt ya.

Mel gets a little braver, moves in closer, almost within JILLY's *reach now. He stretches his neck out toward the feed bucket, sniffing.*

JILLY *(continuing)*: Atsa boy. Atsa good boy. Just take it easy now.

JILLY *slowly brings the halter out from behind her back and starts to move it toward Mel's neck. His ears prick when he sees the halter.*

JILLY (*continuing*): Take it easy.

> JILLY *almost gets the halter strap up to Mel's neck, when he suddenly bolts and goes galloping off into the woods, away from her.*

JILLY (*continuing*): Shit! Mel, you get back here right now! Mel! I hate horses! Mel! Mel!

> JILLY *slams the bucket into a tree, then tromps off into the woods after Mel.*

CUT TO:

EXTERIOR. TWO-LANE COUNTRY HIGHWAY—LATE AFTERNOON.

INTERIOR. CAR—KATE DRIVING. She clutches the wheel and talks to herself intensely as she drives. The road is bordered by thick birch and aspen. There's not a car to be seen in either direction.

KATE: You line up the little bead—no, no, yeah, yeah. You line up the little bead in front with the "V" in the back.

> *She slams the wheel with the palm of her hand.*

KATE (*continuing*): Oh, God. I can't do this! I CAN'T DO THIS, DAD!! Goddamn you. Goddamn you for asking me to do this! You did it on purpose, too, didn't you? I mean you knew I wouldn't be able to do it. It's another one of your tests, right? It's another one of your stupid tests! Like throwing me off the end of the dock.

CUT TO:

QUICK FLASHBACK TO BERTRUM as a younger man, throwing KATE as a naked baby off the end of a dock into a lake.

(Note: Each of these flashbacks in this series should have the authenticity of old 8mm home movies from the fifties, i.e., hand-held, faster speed, radically fluctuating light exposures, and silent.)

CUT BACK TO:

KATE: You remember that one? Or putting me up bareback on
   wild ponies?

QUICK FLASHBACK—BERTRUM, *middle-aged, slaps a
mangy pony on the ass with a switch and laughs uproariously as
little* KATE *hangs on to the mane for dear life. The pony bucks
wildly.*

CUT BACK TO:

KATE: Oh, how 'bout the time you let me drive that old John
   Deere straight into a tree before you showed me where the
   brakes were? Remember? How 'bout that one?

QUICK FLASHBACK—BERTRUM *older and* KATE *as an ado-
lescent. She drives a big John Deere tractor straight into a tree.*
BERTRUM *doubles over with laughter, makes a face to the camera.*

CUT BACK TO:

KATE STILL DRIVING—*clutching the wheel. She stares
straight down the empty road and continues talking to her absent
father.*

KATE: You remember all those tests, Dad? Well, lemme tell you
   something, Dad—Lemme tell ya one thing right now. They
   never did me a damn bit a' good. I mean, I learned to swim
   on my own! I learned to ride on my own! And I learned—
   Well, I never did learn to drive a tractor. But it doesn't
   matter. I mean the fact is that none of your tests did me a
   damn bit of good. Not one of 'em! The only thing it taught
   me was how to fight back! So I guess I owe you for that. But
   I'm not gonna shoot your horse! I'm not shootin' your
   goddamn horse! You can shoot him yourself!

*KATE'S POINT OF VIEW. Suddenly, Mel comes blasting out
of the woods, by the edge of the road, not more than thirty yards
from her car, heading straight for the road.*

ANGLE ON KATE—*sudden panic*—*can't believe her eyes.
She mashes down on the brake pedal.*

LONG SHOT—CRANE—ABOVE ROAD.

KATE'S CAR SWERVING AWAY FROM CAMERA,
screeching rubber, barely missing Mel, who escapes to the other side
of road and disappears into the woods again. Kate's car spins in a
complete circle, steadies, then slumps off the shoulder and into a
ditch. Car stops dead.

HOLD ON LONG SHOT.

Total stillness except for sounds from the woods—owl, birds, frog,
etc. Just Kate's car sitting there at an angle in the ditch.

Mel reappears, after a moment. He peeks out from the woods and
stares across the road at Kate's car.

STILL IN LONG SHOT.

Kate's door opens slowly, then we see her leg emerge—then an arm.
Mel just stands there, across the road, watching her intently.

MEDIUM ANGLE ON KATE as she extricates herself from
the car but keeps her eyes peeled on Mel the whole time, as though
half believing he might be an apparition.

KATE'S POINT OF VIEW ON MEL across the road, staring
straight at her. He snorts and moves toward her direction a few
strides.

CLOSE ON KATE standing, stunned, by the door of the car.

KATE: Oh, Mel! What're you doin' here? Go on, go on, get outta
here. Mel, go on, beat it!! Don't you have any sense?!

ANGLE ON KATE as fear creeps into her face.

KATE: I'm not kidding, Mel! You don't understand something!
I'm the one who's supposed to shoot you! God.

ANGLE ON MEL, now without the X, back to normal. He
starts walking straight toward KATE.

LONG SHOT to see Mel crossing the road toward KATE, *on the other side. Mel walks straight up to* KATE *and stops directly in front of her. STILL IN LONG SHOT.*

KATE *(continuing)*: Oh, brother. You're a dumb horse, aren't you? Really, really dumb. What am I gonna do now?

CUT TO:

INTERIOR. AMY'S KITCHEN—DUSK.

RITA *is getting herself dressed for the outdoors. She moves stiffly from the fall off the horse and favors her back in a slightly melodramatic way. Again, the sense of her pride being injured more than her body.*

RITA: Why didn't I catch it myself? I should have done it myself. She's no good with horses.

AMY: I wouldn't worry too much, honey. Jilly knows the woods.

RITA: Not like she used to. She's a teenager now. She doesn't know anything like she used to. She gets lost in her own bedroom now.

Car lights sweep across the windows. Sound of a car approaching outside, on gravel driveway.

AMY: There, see? Somebody's found her, I bet. She probably walked out to the road and hitched a ride.

RITA *limps toward the front door with* AMY *right behind her.*

RITA: I've told her a thousand times not to hitchhike!

CUT TO:

EXTERIOR. KATE'S CAR—SAME TIME—DUSK.

The car is coming slowly up the driveway with Mel trotting right along beside. KATE's *arm is seen hanging out the window, holding the reins, as they head toward the house.*

REVERSE ANGLE ON RITA AND AMY coming out onto front porch, staring at the approaching car and Mel.

ANGLE ON KATE'S CAR as it pulls to a stop in the yard. KATE *gets out, gives Mel a pat on the neck, then waves to* AMY *and* RITA *with a big smile.*

KATE *(all smiles)*: Look! I found Mel! I almost hit him with the car. He was right out on the road!

CLOSE ON RITA, mean eyes—she is burning at KATE. *She moves off the porch toward* KATE, *really demonstrating her limp now, for* KATE's *benefit.* AMY *follows her, off the porch.*

AMY: What was he doing on the road? That's no place for a horse.

CLOSE ON KATE seeing RITA *heading toward her, fuming mad.*

KATE: Now, look, Rita—before you get excited—I've thought this whole thing out.

KATE'S POINT OF VIEW. RITA *is limping toward her with* AMY *following.*

RITA: Gimme this horse!

WIDE SHOT—INCLUDES ALL THREE WOMEN AND MEL.

KATE: Here. Take him. You can have him. I brought him home for you.

KATE *hands the reins over to* RITA, *who takes Mel and tries to move him close to the car so she can get up on his back by stepping up on the bumper for added height.*

KATE: Lookit, I just wanted to tell you, Rita, that I've changed my mind about the whole thing. Do you hear me?

RITA *refuses to answer* KATE *and keeps trying to maneuver Mel so she can mount him from the car.*

AMY: Rita, you answer your sister.

KATE: We can give him away to someone. We'll give him to somebody in another county and Dad'll never know the difference.

AMY: Of course he won't.

>RITA *finally gets a leg over Mel and grabs his mane and reins. She turns him and heads across the yard for the woods.* KATE *follows her with* AMY *behind.*

KATE: Rita, where are you going?

RITA *(on Mel)*: I'm going to look for my daughter!

>*This is* ALL SHOT ON THE MOVE *with* KATE *and* RITA *following along on foot behind Mel as* RITA *urges him toward the woods.*

KATE: What's happened to Jilly? *(She turns back to* AMY.*)* Where's Jilly, Momma?

AMY: I can't keep track of it anymore. Nobody stays in one place like they used to.

KATE *(back to* RITA*)*: Hey, Rita, wait up! You can't go off in the woods all by yourself! Come on, Rita!

>AMY *stops and watches as she sees* KATE *trying to catch up with Mel and* RITA *as they head into the woods. The full moon is on the rise.*

AMY *(to herself)*: Now they'll all be lost.

>*Their voices fade as they walk toward the woods.*

RITA: She went to look for Mel.

KATE: Mel's right here. Don't go off in the woods by yourself, Rita. Rita!

>*CUT TO:*

>*INTERIOR. HOSPITAL ROOM—CLOSE ON TV SCREEN—NIGHT.*

Horse racing—a review of the day's races with the announcer's voice-over.

ANGLE ON UNCLE DANE sitting on the edge of Bertrum's bed, watching the races. He slides the bottle of rum down from inside his sleeve, takes a belt, then tucks the bottle back up his sleeve. BERTRUM *is still on oxygen, lying in bed, eyes closed.*

CLOSE ON TV as the horses hit the top of the stretch, going for home.

ANGLE ON UNCLE DANE as he leaps off Bertrum's bed and starts yelling at the television.

UNCLE DANE: Come on, keep goin', keep goin', come on, come on. . . . Drop the hammer on him, Miguel! Drop the hammer! Don't pull on his mouth!

BERTRUM *sits up fast in bed, ripping the oxygen off his face and stares around the room, completely disoriented.* UNCLE DANE *remains involved in the horse race for a moment until he realizes* BERTRUM *has come to life.*

UNCLE DANE *(continuing; to* BERTRUM*)*: He's holding him! You see that? He's holding the *sonofabitch!*

Now UNCLE DANE *suddenly realizes that* BERTRUM *is sitting up.*

UNCLE DANE *(continuing)*: Hey! Bertrum! What're you doin', Bertrum? Yer supposed to keep that oxygen stuff on. You gotta stay hooked up on that thing.

UNCLE DANE *makes a vain attempt to hook* BERTRUM *back up to the equipment, but* BERTRUM *shoves him away. He seems to, miraculously, have all the strength in the world now.*

BERTRUM: You stay clear a' me!

UNCLE DANE: Yer gonna die without air, Bertrum. You're in critical condition.

BERTRUM *turns and stares out the window at the lake.*

BERTRUM: What's that?

UNCLE DANE *eyes him, warily.*

UNCLE DANE: What's what?

BERTRUM: That, out there.

ANGLE ON LAKE SUPERIOR, tanker cruising by.

UNCLE DANE: That's Lake Superior, Bertrum. It always has been.

BERTRUM: Oh.

BERTRUM *suddenly drops the whole concern, turns away from window, and stares around the room.*

BERTRUM *(continuing)*: Where's Kate?

UNCLE DANE: Kate? She's at home, I guess.

BERTRUM: What's she doin' at home? I could die here and she's at home?

UNCLE DANE: This is a hospital, Bertrum. They take care of you in a hospital. It's the best place to be if you die. Come on.

BERTRUM *stands abruptly.*

BERTRUM: This is a hospital!

UNCLE DANE: Yes. You got yer bell rung pretty good. Don't you remember?

BERTRUM: This is a hospital?

UNCLE DANE: Right.

BERTRUM: This is a hospital!?

UNCLE DANE: Now, come on, Bertrum.

BERTRUM: This is a hospital!?!

UNCLE DANE: Yes.

BERTRUM *lumbers across the room in search of his clothes.* UNCLE DANE *follows.*

BERTRUM: Well, what am I doing in a hospital? Where's my clothes? I got business to take care of. Nobody else is gonna do it. Kate's not gonna do it, that's for sure.

UNCLE DANE: No, no, no, no. You can't walk outta here, Bertrum. They're not gonna let you do that. Bertrum!

BERTRUM: Gimme my clothes!!! Gimme my clothes!!! I got a job to do.

UNCLE DANE: You're hooked up to this thing. Come on!

BERTRUM: That horse is not gonna get away with this.

UNCLE DANE: Well, take your boots. Bertrum, you can't just go out like this. Bertrum, wait up! Bertrum, wait up!

DANE *looks back at the TV and moans; he's missing the race.*

ON TV AS RACE CONTINUES.

EXTERIOR: OUTSKIRTS OF DULUTH—NIGHT.

Abandoned neighborhood on the edge of the city. Two-story brick and wood-frame houses line a wide broken blacktop road. The houses are built right to the edge of the road with no sidewalk, like those seen in many old mining towns. All the buildings are a shambles, mostly boarded up, broken windows, peeling paint, and caved-in roofs. The streetlights still work and are the old-fashioned globe type that hang out over the road on telephone poles. A train is heard in the distance. The moan of a tugboat.

UNCLE DANE and BERTRUM are seen, at a long distance, walking down the empty road TOWARD CAMERA. BERTRUM is plodding determinedly along in his hospital smock with a blanket thrown over his shoulders, holding the corners tight around his neck. He has long johns on, his work boots, and his railroad cap. UNCLE DANE

*has his overcoat thrown over his hospital smock with the rum bottle
hanging halfway out of one of the pockets. He wears long johns with
his hospital slippers on and his cap.*

UNCLE DANE *is slightly behind* BERTRUM *but trying to keep pace.*

UNCLE DANE: If they catch you, Bertrum, they're just gonna toss
you back in there. You know that, don't you? *(Pause.)* Have
you got any idea how many miles it is from the hospital to
your place? Have you got a rough estimate in yer mind or
are you just hoping for the best?

BERTRUM *doesn't answer, just keeps grimly walking, eyes set on the
road ahead. They keep coming CLOSER TO CAMERA.*

UNCLE DANE *(continuing)*: We could still be walkin' by morning,
Bertrum? We could walk all through the night! And still not
be there!

BERTRUM *stops abruptly and turns to* UNCLE DANE, *who also
stops.*

BERTRUM: If you don't shut up, I'm gonna find a large rock and
beat you to death with it! Now, git away from me!

UNCLE DANE: There aren't any large rocks. This is the city. It's
what I'm trying to tell you. We're in the city here!

BERTRUM: You ignorant numbskull!

BERTRUM *turns back and continues walking down the road, toward
camera.* UNCLE DANE *follows. As they reach camera and pass it,
the camera pivots and moves with them on their backs for the rest
of the scene.* DANE *takes his bottle out and has a belt as he continues
walking.*

UNCLE DANE: You never listen to reason, Bertrum. That's your
whole trouble. Yer always gonna beat somethin' to death.
Shootin' yer horse ain't gonna solve anything. What's that
gonna solve? All you'll have is a dead horse on yer hands.
Sign that yer losin'. Thing is—thing of it is, yer never gonna

make it. They'll find you by the side of the road, bloated up like an old groundhog!

BERTRUM: I'll make it. All you gotta do is follow these tracks. I know these tracks like the back of my hand.

They have now left the outskirts behind them and head into the country, still following the road but along an embankment that drops steeply down on the railroad tracks. They follow the railroad tracks above. SHOT OF DANE AND BERTRUM walking in the railroad tracks.

CUT TO:

EXTERIOR. WOODS, LAKE, FREIGHT TRAIN, BIRCH TREES—DUSK.

KATE *(voice-over)*: So, you think it's just a superstition, then?

Slowly, silhouetted against the full moon and the black woods, Mel emerges on the horizon from camera left—plodding along with RITA and KATE riding him double. They ride straight across the frame on the same path that JILLY and the BOY took.

RITA *(voice-over) (into SYNC)*: Well, yeah. I mean, that's like believing that if you listen to Beethoven when you're preg-nant that the kid's gonna automatically be born a genius. Why? You're not pregnant, are you?

KATE: Yeah, I think I am.

RITA: Katie! You're pregnant! Why didn't you tell anybody?

KATE: Well, Dad knows. He knows everything.

RITA: So, you're gonna have it, then?

KATE: Yeah. Of course I want to have it. Why wouldn't I have it?

RITA: I don't know.

KATE: What's the pain like?

Suddenly an ear-shattering moan of sexual ecstasy from JILLY *breaks the stillness of the woods.*

TIGHT TWO-SHOT ON RITA AND KATE. They are both frozen by the sound of the scream, then RITA *realizes who it is.*

RITA: JILLLYYYYYYY!!!!!

RITA kicks Mel into a gallop and they go loping OFF-CAMERA RIGHT.

CLOSE ON JILLY with the BOY *on top of her, under a tree. She hears her mother's voice and pushes the* BOY *off, struggling to get out from under him.*

JILLY: Get off! Get offa me!! That's my mom.

They are both sweating like dogs in heat. She takes off, running through the woods in her bra and jeans.

CUT TO:

EXTERIOR. BRIDGE.

BERTRUM and DANE *cross a bridge, silhouetted by blue night, full moon above them.*

BERTRUM: Trouble with you, Dane, see, is that you're never going to be a leader of men. That's your big problem, you're too soft. You gotta learn to look life in the face and not knuckle under. Not run to the goddamn bottle every time you lose on the ponies. Man's a fool to throw his money away on horses anyway. A horse is not an animal to be trusted. You can mark my words on that!

CUT TO:

EXTERIOR. WOODS—NIGHT.

Loon gliding through the water. Giant full moon rising over the trees.

CUT TO:

OWL LANDING ON A TREE BRANCH.

CUT TO:

EXTERIOR. BIRCH FOREST REFLECTING MOON-LIGHT—SAME NIGHT.

The sounds of JILLY *whimpering softly as Mel stomps along through the woods, carrying all three women now.* RITA *at the reins,* JILLY *in the middle, and* KATE *behind.* JILLY *is trying to pull on the last of her clothing that was salvaged from the woods. She keeps sobbing to herself as* KATE *tries to console her from behind.*

KATE: What were you doin' out here with a strange boy anyway, Jilly?

RITA: Oh, Jilly, just stop that whimpering, will you?! We spent half the night searching around for your clothes. You've got no right to whimper.

JILLY *(through her sobs):* All I wanna do is have some fun! Nobody in this family wants to have any fun! You're all nuts!

RITA: Jilly, if you don't stop it right now, I'm gonna put you back on the ground and you can walk home.

JILLY: Good! Good! I wanna get off this horse! I want to get off this fucking horse. I never asked to be put on this fucking horse.

RITA: You watch your language!

JILLY *struggles to jump off Mel as* KATE *holds on to her from behind.*

KATE: Take it easy, Jilly. You're gonna hurt yourself.

JILLY: Let go a' me! I'm not your prisoner!

RITA: You're not getting off this horse until we get home!

JILLY: I wish I was dead!!!

JILLY *gives up struggling and just weeps.*

CUT TO:

EXTERIOR. NIGHT.

BERTRUM *and* UNCLE DANE *walking on the tracks (action same as earlier).*

UNCLE DANE: Have you ever thought about what yer gonna do once ya shoot yer only horse!

BERTRUM *stops dead in his tracks and turns back to* UNCLE DANE, *who also stops.* CAMERA STOPS WITH THEM.

CLOSE ON BERTRUM glaring at DANE.

CLOSE ON UNCLE DANE.

UNCLE DANE: Who's gonna pull yer buckboard then?

WIDE TWO-SHOT: BERTRUM *leans over and finds a big rock.* UNCLE DANE *starts to retreat.* BERTRUM *rears back and unleashes the rock at* UNCLE DANE, *who slips backward and crashes down the embankment, ass over teakettle, to the railroad tracks below.* BER- TRUM *stares in* DANE's *direction for a moment, then turns and continues doggedly on down the road.*

BERTRUM: Just the ticket. Just the ticket. I warned ya, I warned ya. Run! Run, you goddamn fink. Goddamn relatives.

CUT TO:

INTERIOR. GRAMMA'S KITCHEN—SAME NIGHT.

CLOSE ON A CALENDAR. On Gramma's table, GRAMMA's *bony finger traces the days of the week and stops on Sunday. She taps the date with her long fingernail.*

ANGLE ON GRAMMA sitting alone at her kitchen table, staring down at the calendar. Her face slowly rises and she stares up at the ceiling.

GRAMMA: Nobody'll be there.

CUT TO:

EXTERIOR. WOODS—SAME NIGHT.

KATE, JILLY, RITA *on the horse.*

RITA: Don't you say that! Don't you ever say anything like that! That's an insult to me and everyone else in this family.

JILLY: Well, this family is an insult to me!

Pause. KATE *rubs* JILLY'*s back, speaks softly to her as* JILLY *tries to control her sobbing.* RITA *urges Mel forward through the woods.*

KATE: You'll only wish you were dead for another year or so. Then it'll all change, honey. Wait and see. It'll all be different once you get out of here.

JILLY: I'll never get outta here.

KATE *leans forward and whispers in* JILLY'S *ear.*

KATE: Did you use any protection?

RITA *reaches back and taps* KATE *on the head.*

CUT TO:

EXTERIOR. REMOTE RAILROAD TRACKS CUTTING THROUGH FOREST—SAME NIGHT.

ANGLE ON BERTRUM as he dodges UNCLE DANE'*s empty rum bottle. The bottle barely misses his head and shatters on a boulder behind him.*

ANGLE ON UNCLE DANE heading down the tracks toward BERTRUM, *his pockets loaded with old empty beer bottles and large rocks.*

UNCLE DANE: Close! That was close! Next one's gonna take yer head off, Bertrum! Take it clean off at the neck!

BERTRUM: You've lost your mind.

ANGLE ON BERTRUM stumbling across the tracks in retreat. He heads straight for the woods, trying to get out of UNCLE DANE's *range.*

UNCLE DANE *in hot pursuit, a beer bottle in each hand. He lobs them at* BERTRUM *as though they were hand grenades.*

UNCLE DANE: This one's got your name on it, Bertrum! "Moose Head"!! Might as well give up the ghost!!

BERTRUM: You're crazy!

UNCLE DANE: I'm crazy, all right. Now it's your turn to run! Run, you bastard! Run!

BERTRUM: You maniac!

UNCLE DANE: Gotcha!

CUT TO:

EXTERIOR. DEEP WOODS—SAME NIGHT.

Mel, still plodding along with the three women on his back. JILLY *is slumped over in a deep sleep, her head bobbing. She is squeezed between* RITA *and* KATE. KATE *supports* JILLY *from behind.*

KATE: Are you sure Mel can find his way home, Rita?

RITA: He's never failed on me yet.

KATE: Yeah, but that was a long time ago. You haven't ridden him out here since you were a kid.

RITA: The woods haven't changed. They're the same woods. He can smell the barn from miles away.

KATE: I hope so.

RITA: Don't worry. He's a good horse. Aren't ya, Mel.

RITA *reaches down and pats Mel on the neck. They keep moving through the woods.*

KATE: Oh, I know he's a good horse. I mean I have no doubt he's a good horse. It just seems like we've been out in these woods an awful long time now. Momma's gonna wonder what happened to us.

RITA: He'll find his way. You wait and see.

CUT TO:

INTERIOR. HOUSE.

AMY *at kitchen table, looking at photos.*

AMY: Lord have mercy.

CUT TO:

ANGLE ON BERTRUM—STILL IN WOODS.

He is crashing into the woods as a beer bottle zings past his ear and smashes into a tree. BERTRUM *lumbers through the brush, looking for cover. He stops briefly now and then to pick up a good-sized throwing rock and stashes it in his blanket, storing up ammo for the ensuing battle. He keeps moving through the woods, peering back over his shoulder for* DANE.

DANE: You can kiss tomorrow good-bye, Bertrum!

BERTRUM *(to himself)*: It's in the blood, that's what it is, bad blood. Mentally deficient. Shoulda known that from the get-go. Her whole side of the family. That Nordic blood. That's what it is. Deranged.

CUT TO:

INTERIOR. GRAMMA'S KITCHEN.

GRAMMA *at the kitchen table, singing a Finnish tune.*

CUT BACK TO:

EXTERIOR. BERTRUM IN THE WOODS.

BERTRUM *(to himself)*: You could see it in her eyes a long time ago.

QUICK CUT TO:

AMY'S EYES IN TIGHT CLOSEUP from the photograph of her as a young woman. BERTRUM*'s voice carries over this image, then . . .*

RETURNS TO:

EXTERIOR. WOODS.

BERTRUM *is struggling through the woods, pursued by* DANE.

BERTRUM: Every one of 'em had the same mark. Every single one of 'em. Those slanty eyes. Mongolian! The hordes! Invaded by barbarians.

Another beer bottle whistles past BERTRUM*'s head and shatters against a tree.* BERTRUM *presses on.* DANE *howls fiercely from behind.*

ANGLE ON DANE.

ANGLE ON BERTRUM.

BERTRUM: That's where they got it! The tribes! Mongols! Just look at her mother, if you don't believe me!

QUICK CUT TO:

GRAMMA'S EYES IN CLOSEUP, THEN SHOT OF HER at the table, still singing. Then . . .

BACK TO:

BERTRUM.

BERTRUM: Nobody in their right mind would marry into eyes like that. They've all got it. They keep passing it on like some disease. BARBARIAN WOMEN!!!

An eerie high shrieking call of a loon, very close and sustained.

CUT TO:

KATE'S EYES IN CLOSEUP, THEN FAST MON-TAGE of different sets of eyes, starting with AMY's *from the photo, then* AMY's *as she is now; then* GRAMMA's *eyes, then* JILLY's, *and ending with* RITA's. *Each pair of eyes fills the frame in extreme closeup. Each painted. HOLD ON RITA'S EYES. The loon call sustains through all this and ends abruptly with:*

PULL BACK FAST ON RITA'S EYES to see RITA *perched at the very top of a tall pine tree, scouting the surrounding area. The full moon behind her.*

ANGLE ON KATE AND JILLY still mounted on Mel, waiting for RITA *at the base of the tree.* JILLY *is sound asleep with her arms around Mel's neck.* KATE *stares up at* RITA *and yells to her.*

KATE: See anything?!

STAY ON KATE with RITA's *voice-over from top of tree.*

RITA *(offscreen)*: No!

KATE: God, we can't be that far away, Rita! Look all around!

RITA *(offscreen)*: I am looking all around! What do you think I'm doing up here anyhow?

KATE: How 'bout the radio tower? Can you see the radio station tower?

RITA *(offscreen)*: No!

JILLY wakes up. She sits straight up on Mel and looks around bleary-eyed, surprised to find herself still in the woods.

JILLY: What's going on?

KATE: We're trying to find our way outta here.

JILLY: Where's Mom?

KATE: She's at the top of this pine tree.

JILLY stares up into the tall pine and squints her eyes.

JILLY: Oh.

JILLY lies back down and falls asleep, hugging Mel's neck. KATE *continues yelling up at* RITA.

KATE: Isn't there anything you can recognize, Rita? What about the grain elevator?

ANGLE ON RITA at the top of the tree, staring down into a clearing in the distance.

RITA'S POINT OF VIEW. She sees BERTRUM *at a distance, lumbering across the clearing with his hospital blanket flapping. It's too far away for her to recognize him as anything more than a figure in the moonlight.*

CLOSE ON RITA, eyes wide. KATE'S *voice is heard from below.*

KATE *(offscreen)*: Rita! Answer me!

RITA: There's somebody out there!

KATE *(offscreen)*: What?

RITA: I just saw somebody go running across that clearing out there! I think he's wearing a cape!

KATE *(offscreen)*: Well, yell to him!

RITA: I'm not gonna yell to him! He's wearing a cape!

KATE *(offscreen)*: Rita, we're lost.

RITA: Well, I'm not gonna yell to him. That's crazy. That could be anybody out there.

RITA'S POINT OF VIEW—DISTANT SHOT OF THE OPEN CLEARING. Now she sees UNCLE DANE *run across the field, hot on the trail of* BERTRUM, *his overcoat flapping behind him.*

ANGLE ON RITA.

RITA: There's two of them!

ANGLE ON KATE yelling at the top of her lungs.

KATE: Heeeeeeeeeeeeelp!!!!!!!

JILLY wakes up with a start and almost falls off Mel. KATE *hangs on to her.*

JILLY: What's wrong?

CUT TO:

EXTERIOR. WOODS. AT THE EDGE OF THE CLEARING.

ANGLE ON UNCLE DANE as he comes to a screeching halt, hearing the echo of KATE's *cry for help. He just stands there, frozen to the spot, listening intently to the woods. Silence except for the pervasive humming of insects.* UNCLE DANE's *eyes widen with apprehension.*

ANGLE ON BERTRUM a little deeper in the woods, also frozen, having heard the scream from KATE. *He listens to the woods with the same intensity as* DANE. *After a moment he calls out to* DANE.

BERTRUM: Dane? *(Pause.)* That you?

ANGLE ON UNCLE DANE.

UNCLE DANE: I'm headin' for the highway, Bertrum! I don't know about you!

UNCLE DANE turns and sprints back across the field in the direction he came from.

ANGLE ON BERTRUM, also running, trying to catch up with DANE.

KATE *(offscreen)*: HEEEEEEEEEEEEEEEELP!!!!!!!!!!

BERTRUM *(at a run)*: Which way is the highway? Wait up! Just hang on a second, Dane!

Another piercing scream from KATE *resounds through the forest, echoing off every tree.*

LONG SHOT OF BERTRUM AND UNCLE DANE running for all they are worth back across the clearing, blanket and overcoat flapping in the moonlight.

CUT TO:

EXTERIOR. DEEP WOODS—FULL MOON—NIGHT.

RITA *jumps down from the pine tree, beside Mel.* KATE *and* JILLY, *still mounted on Mel.*

RITA: Stop that screaming! Jesus! Here we are, three women, alone, out in the middle of nowhere and you're screaming at strange men with capes!

KATE: We're lost, Rita! We've been lost for hours now.

JILLY *(drowsy)*: We're lost? I thought we were going home?

RITA: We *are* going home. All we gotta do is let Mel find his way back. We just need a little patience now.

KATE: Well, how much time does Mel need? A week, maybe?

RITA: He can do it.

JILLY: How long have we been lost?

KATE: Mel couldn't find his own tail! He doesn't know his ass from a hole in the ground! He was lost when I found him out there on the road—fifty yards from the house!

JILLY: Did we bring any food?

RITA: He's a good horse!

KATE: Oh, shut up about "he's a good horse"! I don't wanna hear "he's a good horse" anymore, Rita. He's dumb as a post. And I'm not lettin' him take us any deeper into the woods.

KATE slides down off Mel's back, leaving JILLY alone on him.

JILLY: Don't leave me up here!

RITA: He's not dumb!

KATE: He's an idiot! And you're an idiot for thinking he'll find his way home!

JILLY: Don't leave me up here! I don't know how to ride!

RITA: Just hang on to his mane, Jilly.

JILLY: I don't know how to ride!

KATE storms off, walking straight into the woods, away from them.

RITA: Kate! Kate! Where are you going?

KATE *(not turning back)*: I'm walkin'!

RITA: Katie, get back here! We've gotta stick together now!

JILLY: Don't leave me on this horse!

CUT TO:

EXTERIOR. WOODS—SAME NIGHT.

BERTRUM *and* UNCLE DANE *striding side by side now. They are beginning to crap out from all the running. They blow and gasp for air.*

KATE's *voice echoing through the trees:*

KATE *(offscreen)*: HEEEEEEEEEEEEELP!!!!!

Immediately, BERTRUM *and* UNCLE DANE *pick up their pace. They are shoulder to shoulder now. Tracking with them in profile.*

UNCLE DANE: That's a woman's voice, right?

BERTRUM: Sounds like a woman to me.

UNCLE DANE: Uh— Maybe we oughta go see what the trouble is, Bertrum.

BERTRUM: I don't wanna know what the trouble is. I got plenty of my own.

UNCLE DANE: Yeah, but I mean—maybe she's getting—about to be murdered or something.

BERTRUM: And what're you gonna do about it, Mr. Hero?

CUT TO:

EXTERIOR. WOODS—SAME NIGHT.

*MOVING SHOT—*RITA *trying to catch up with* KATE, *on foot, crashing through the woods. Both women striding fast. The pace is hot and furious.*

RITA: So, that's the way things are, huh? When the chips are down, you just walk off and leave us. Jump ship!

KATE: I'm findin' a way outta here! I'm not gonna wander around on that worthless horse all night.

RITA: You never did like Mel, did you?

KATE: Oh, stop being so pathetic, Rita! You act like you gave birth to that damn horse!

RITA: You woulda shot him, wouldn't you? If you'd'a known how to use a gun, you woulda shot him!

KATE: Okay, yeah! Yeah, I woulda shot him! How's that!

RITA: Just to piss me off! Just outta spite! You're worse than Dad!

KATE: Well, at least I paid him a visit! At least I brought him some lemon drops! That's more'n I can say for you! You never even gave him a call!

RITA: You've always been on his side, haven't you?

KATE: I can appreciate his point of view!

CUT TO:

DANE *and* BERTRUM *panting, walking through the woods.*

BACK TO:

RITA: Always lookin' down on me and Momma and everyone else! Big City Career Girl!

KATE: Oh, yeah, beats livin' at home with Momma!

RITA: Now you've got yourself knocked up and you don't even have a man, do ya, Kate?

KATE: Where's your man, Rita?

RITA: I don't need a man!

KATE *suddenly turns on* RITA *and starts coming after her.* RITA *turns and runs.*

KATE: I'm gonna belt you. I'm gonna belt you right across the head!

RITA *(on the run)*: Why don't you shoot me instead?!

KATE: You *better* run, sister!

QUICK CUT TO:

Mel galloping, out of control, through the woods, reins flapping, with JILLY *hanging onto his neck for dear life. She screams:*

JILLY: HEEEEEEEEEEEEELP!!!!!

CUT TO:

EXTERIOR. EMPTY TWO-LANE HIGHWAY—BOR-DERED BY WOODS—SAME NIGHT.

JILLY's *screams overlap onto* BERTRUM *and* UNCLE DANE, *desperately trying to keep running down the middle of the highway. They are both gasping for air.*

UNCLE DANE: There's two of 'em! That was a different voice, Bertrum!

BERTRUM: Just keep movin'! Keep it movin'!

UNCLE DANE: I'm runnin' outta air, Bertrum!

BERTRUM and UNCLE DANE slow down to a walk, blowing hard. They come to a full stop in the middle of the road, bending at the waist with their hands on their knees and gasping for air. They speak to each other in this position between breaths.

BERTRUM: This is all on account a' that damn horse, ya know. That horse is at the root of this whole mess.

UNCLE DANE: I don't see how you can blame a horse for us being lost out on the highway.

BERTRUM: He started the whole thing.

UNCLE DANE sees headlights coming from a distance, toward them. He straightens up, still breathing hard. BERTRUM stays doubled over.

UNCLE DANE: There's a car comin'! Maybe we can flag him down, Bertrum. There's a car! Look!

BERTRUM takes a glance at the oncoming headlights but remains bent over at the waist, gulping air.

BERTRUM: So what?

UNCLE DANE: Start wavin' your hands! Wave your arms, Bertrum!

UNCLE DANE starts waving his arms wildly at the oncoming car. BERTRUM stays bent over. They're both in the middle of the road.

BERTRUM: *You* wave yer arms! I'm about to have a heart attack here!

UNCLE DANE keeps waving madly, but the car keeps coming straight at them at them at the same speed.

UNCLE DANE: He's not slowing down!

BERTRUM: Don't matter. I'm ready to die.

UNCLE DANE *takes ahold of* BERTRUM'*s shoulder to pull him off the road, but* BERTRUM *pushes him away and remains in the middle of the road.*

UNCLE DANE: Come on, we better get off the road, Bertrum! Whatsa matter with you? He's not slowing down!

BERTRUM: Let him come!

UNCLE DANE: He's comin' right for us, Bertrum!

BERTRUM: You better run.

UNCLE DANE'S POINT OF VIEW of car getting closer and closer.

DANE *gives a look to* BERTRUM, *then runs for the shoulder of the road, leaving* BERTRUM, *still bent over, hands on his knees.*

CLOSE ON BERTRUM staring down the road at the headlights, which are getting closer. He slowly straightens himself up to a standing position, facing the charging car, then slowly raises his arm high over his head and gives the car the finger. He just holds this position rigidly, like a statue. He speaks to himself but also to the anonymous car.

CLOSE ON UNCLE DANE lying on his belly, off the shoulder of the road, watching BERTRUM *and the approaching car. He yells to* BERTRUM *but* BERTRUM *is immovable.*

UNCLE DANE: Bertrum! This is not an honorable way to die! Nobody's gonna remember this! Yer just gonna get squashed like a toad! Bertrum!

BERTRUM: This is for Korea, sucker! And the railroad, and everything else that happened before you were born!

UNCLE DANE'S POINT OF VIEW. BERTRUM *is steadfast, holding his position with his finger raised high at the speeding car.*

The car horn blares and stays on a continuous note as the car heads straight toward the unyielding BERTRUM.

BERTRUM'S POINT OF VIEW. The car is heading directly toward him, headlights blinking, horn blaring. The car swerves at the last second and misses him by inches, tires screaming, then continues on down the road with the horn still blaring and fading into the distance.

BERTRUM *never moves an inch through all this. He remains there with his finger still raised high, like a military statue.*

CLOSE ON UNCLE DANE, wild-eyed, splattered with mud, half buried by the side of the road. He stares at BERTRUM.

ANGLE ON BERTRUM still standing like a statue with his finger up in the air. He squints at something down the road, in the distance.

BERTRUM'S POINT OF VIEW. Way down the road, in the middle of the yellow line, can be seen the image of Mel emerging, with the three women on his back, heading straight toward BER-TRUM. *At first, the image is slightly blurred and silent, like a dream, shimmering in moonlight.*

CLOSE ON BERTRUM still frozen. He blinks his eyes hard and tries to focus on the vision.

BERTRUM'S POINT OF VIEW. Now Mel and the women can be made out more clearly. They are getting closer. The sound of Mel's hooves on the blacktop.

CLOSE ON BERTRUM. His breathing becomes rapid. Sweat breaks out on his forehead. He starts to shake and tremble but keeps staring down the road and holding his position. He tries to speak to DANE, *but nothing comes out.*

The high shrill sound of a loon is accompanied by the shrieks of all three women, but now they sound like barbarian hordes in full battle. The thundering of Mel's hooves getting closer.

BERTRUM'S POINT OF VIEW. He sees a nightmare approaching. Mel has the white X painted on his face and he's in full gallop, sparks flying from his hooves. The women are all in primitive warpaint; strips of rawhide with skulls tied to them clatter around their waists. They brandish sickles and lances with banners streaming from them. They carry knives between their teeth. They scream savagely like demons from hell as they swoop down on BERTRUM.

CLOSE ON BERTRUM. He is shaking violently, frothing at the mouth, sweat rolling down his cheeks but still refusing to move an inch from his stance.

ANGLE ON UNCLE DANE pulling himself up from the side of the road and staggering toward BERTRUM.

UNCLE DANE: Bertrum? Bertrum?

CLOSE ON BERTRUM. He speaks to DANE.

BERTRUM: That's my horse! That's the horse that tried to kill me! He's comin' for me, Dane! He's comin' to take me away!!!

BERTRUM *drops suddenly to the blacktop in an unconscious heap.*

UNCLE DANE: Bertrum? Bertrum?

ANGLE ON UNCLE DANE seeing BERTRUM *fall, then seeing Mel and the women approach.*

UNCLE DANE'S POINT OF VIEW. He sees Mel and the women in their normal guise, all dressed as themselves and Mel without the X. KATE *pulls Mel right beside* BERTRUM *and she dismounts and approaches* BERTRUM.

UNCLE DANE: Bertrum? Bertrum?

CLOSE ON KATE seeing BERTRUM.

KATE: Dad? Is that Dad?

CUT TO:

EXTERIOR.   HIGHWAY—NEXT   MORNING—
BREAK OF DAY.

The little two-lane highway is completely empty. Mel is walking
straight down the middle of it with BERTRUM *slumped across his*
back, belly down and completely out. The three women walk along
in front of Mel, KATE *holding the reins.* UNCLE DANE *limps along*
in the rear, singing wearily to himself, holding on to the horse's tail.
They all look as though they've been walking for hours.

UNCLE DANE:
Camptown races, five miles long,
Doo-dah, doo-dah,
Camptown races, five miles long,
All the doo-dah day (etc.)

ANGLE ON AMY standing in the middle of the road in her black
dress, standing exactly as she was in the old photo, seeing the group
approach, at a distance.

ANGLE ON KATE smiling at her.

AMY'S POINT OF VIEW of Mel and the whole group again,
getting closer, with UNCLE DANE *continuing his song.*

CUT TO:

INTERIOR. GRAMMA'S HOUSE—MIDMORNING.

A large throng of women gathered around Gramma's living room
table for her birthday. They all sing a Finnish song for her. The
remains of a gigantic breakfast on the plates in front of them.
GRAMMA *sits at the head of the table in her wheelchair, facing a*
large chocolate cake with dozens of burning candles. She is sur-
rounded by the family and their children—all girls. Not a man in
sight. Close behind GRAMMA *are* AMY, KATE, RITA, *and* JILLY,
all decked out in party dresses. GRAMMA *wears a pink bow in her*
hair. She seems completely bewildered by the whole event. The

room is overflowing with laughter, conversation, and buoyant female energy. A bottle of champagne is making the rounds. Lots of beer on the table. JILLY *is sloshed again and having a great time. All these women are big-boned, raw, blond country girls with a very definite Nordic similarity among them.*

ANGLE ON KATE as she steps forward to ask for a pause in the festivities. She moves up beside GRAMMA *and puts her hand on* GRAMMA*'s shoulder.* GRAMMA *is still bewildered by it all. Singing, clapping ends.*

KATE: Come on, Gramma, blow out your candles.

GRAMMA: I'm not gonna blow any candles out.

KATE: Oh, come on. We'll all help.

GRAMMA: Candles are stupid.

KATE: Everybody, one . . . two . . . three!

They all help blow candles out. More cheering and clapping.

GRAMMA: God doesn't count the years. Only people count the years. It's stupid.

KATE *(continuing)*: Come on, how about a toast to Gramma.

All the women grab glasses. Lots of pouring and good cheer. They all raise their glasses toward GRAMMA, *who just scowls at them.*

KATE *(continuing)*: To our dearest grandma, Trenje—The Source of Us All!!!

Everyone drinks her champagne, cheers, applause for GRAMMA— *some of the women throw their glasses against the walls.* GRAMMA *is unmoved by it all.*

GRAMMA: Who's gonna clean up the mess?

KATE *(continuing)*: Now, Momma, why don't you give Gramma our present?

AMY: Oh. You bet. This is really from Katie, Ma.

AMY *hands a brightly wrapped gift to* GRAMMA *who shakily starts tearing the ribbon and paper off.*

KATE: Well, it's from all of us.

GRAMMA: Why is everyone here on a Sunday?

AMY: I told you they would be.

GRAMMA: Doesn't anyone go to church?

GRAMMA *pulls the present out of its wrapping and stares at it. It's the photo of Amy and the girls on the pony, now in a bright gold frame.* GRAMMA *stares at it hard, squinting her eyes and holding it way from her gaze.*

GRAMMA *(continuing; staring at photo)*: That's not me, is it?

AMY: No, Momma. It's me and the girls.

GRAMMA *stares hard at the photo.*

GRAMMA: Where's all the men?

CUT TO:

EXTERIOR. A LARGE OPEN FIELD WITH A HILL IN THE DISTANCE—AFTERNOON.

Snow has fallen. In long shot we see BERTRUM *slowly leading Mel away from camera toward the hill. He carries the deer rifle in one hand. Camera holds full frame as* BERTRUM *just keeps walking steadily with Mel behind him, straight toward the distant hill. Finally,* BERTRUM *and Mel reach the hill. They climb it and, slowly, they both disappear over the rise.*

silent tongue

LE STUDIO CANAL +
PRESENTS
A BELBO/ALIVE PRODUCTION

A SAM SHEPARD FILM

ALAN BATES
RICHARD HARRIS
DERMOT MULRONEY
and
RIVER PHOENIX

SILENT TONGUE

SHEILA TOUSEY
JERI ARREDONDO
BILL IRWIN
DAVID SHINER
TIM SCOTT *as The Lone Man*
TANTOO CARDINAL *as Silent Tongue*

Casting Director
JENNIFER SHULL

Costume Designers
VAN BROUGHTON RAMSEY and JIM ECHERD

Production Designer
CARY WHITE

Music Composed By
PATRICK O'HEARN

Medicine Show Music By
THE RED CLAY RAMBLERS

Film Editor
BILL YAHRAUS

Director of Photography
JACK CONROY

Executive Producers
GENE ROSOW
BILL YAHRAUS
JACQUES FANSTEN
SHEP GORDON

Produced By
CAROLYN PFEIFFER and LUDI BOEKEN

Written and Directed By
SAM SHEPARD

EXTERIOR. PRAIRIE—DAY.

1873—Llano Estacado, New Mexico Territory.

A vast, primitive prairie landscape of harsh, flat isolation. Nothing moves but the wind and the buffalo grass.

Emerging from the music are the sounds of tin cans, bird and coyote bones rattling together gently in the wind. A distant hawk.

CAMERA PANS SLOWLY FROM LEFT TO RIGHT as the land goes on forever, stretching out to the horizon in every direction without a tree or a living thing in sight. CAMERA CONTINUES PANNING to reveal smoke snaking out across the sky.

DISSOLVE TO:

EXTERIOR. BURIAL TREE—DAY.

CAMERA MOVES through the branches of a tree. Tied to branches are bones and tin cans. The wind blows them gently.

Slowly, as CAMERA CONTINUES TO PAN, a young half-breed Indian girl's corpse is revealed in EXTREME CLOSEUP, following along the length of the body from the feet to the head. The corpse is mounted on a crude scaffold in the crotch of the tree. It is bound tightly in old ragged cavalry and horse blankets with rope and leather straps encircling it. Feathers and bones are tied onto the ropes. The entire body is contained in the blankets, like a mummy, except for the exposed head, which has a broad white stripe painted across the mouth. Her thick black hair blows gently in the breeze.

The sounds of a raging bonfire push into the foreground, through the music and opening sounds.

CAMERA CONTINUES TO PAN off the corpse into the distant landscape and finally comes to rest on:

TALBOT ROE, *sitting on his haunches, gripping the barrel of an old side-by-side shotgun, the stock propped in the ground between his legs. He is a young white man in his early twenties. His face is drawn and weary—haunted looking. His eyes gaze deep into the bonfire as though locked on an image of the past.*

CAMERA MOVES IN TIGHT on his eyes. On close inspection, something profoundly disturbed is revealed—his eyes dart back and forth trying to follow the flames and his own fractured thoughts. The impression is of a man going mad in terrifying moments and then collecting himself long enough to prepare for the next nightmare.

Sound of a turkey vulture in the distance. TALBOT's *eyes flash from the fire to the sky. He remains stock-still in the same position.*

TALBOT'S POINT OF VIEW. The vulture circling high above, directly over the corpse and the bonfire.

CLOSE ON TALBOT, eyes riveted to the vulture.

TALBOT'S POINT OF VIEW. The vulture descending in lower and lower circles, its great wings riding the air currents, as it moves down to the burial tree.

VERY CLOSE ON TALBOT, his eyes following the vulture like a cat.

TALBOT: Tahteh.

TALBOT'S POINT OF VIEW. The vulture tucking its wings, preparing to land on the corpse—then, suddenly, an explosion from the twelve-gauge and the bird is blown out of the air.

WIDE SHOT ON TALBOT running wildly toward the fallen bird, smoke still curling out of his shotgun. He stops suddenly when he reaches the dead vulture. TALBOT *snatches it up and rips the wings off it, then flings the body into the bonfire.* CAMERA FOLLOWS *the vulture's body as it meets the flames.*

MEDIUM ON TALBOT as he climbs the tree and approaches the corpse, placing the vulture's wings on her chest, then kissing her dead lips.

CUT TO:

EXTERIOR. VAST PRAIRIE—SAME DAY.

(Music over and titles continue over.)

A two-day ride from the burial tree and Talbot.

A lone rider in the distance, at a lope with three other horses in tow, without saddles. One horse carries a small pack of supplies. They are traveling left to right on the screen, all the horses parallel, with the mounted horse slightly ahead of the others. They maintain a relentless hard gallop, as though they've been traveling for hours in this fashion.

CUT TO:

EXTERIOR. RISE (ABOVE MEDICINE SHOW CAMP)—DAY.

*The lone rider approaches—*PRESCOTT ROE, *the father of Talbot.* CAMERA CRANES UP *over his shoulder to reveal a stagecoach on a distant road down below.*

CLOSER ON PRESCOTT. He is well into his sixties but rugged as a boot. His eyes have the kind of inner stillness that comes from dealing with nature and horses and not with human beings. He is an absolute extension of his horses. They all just flow along with him at the gallop.

PRESCOTT *pulls his horses up to a walk and stops them at the edge of a high break and looks down. (Medicine show music over.)*

EXTERIOR. MEDICINE SHOW CAMP—DAY.

CLOSE ON HORSES' HOOVES—the stagecoach comes down the road, and as it turns CAMERA MOVES BACK to reveal a KIOWA WARRIOR *in front of a tepee. Following the stagecoach in the background at all times, CAMERA CONTINUES past a* FIRE-EATER, *past a theatrical stage where two* LITTLE PERSON ACROBATS *juggle, accompanied by a band. Still following the stagecoach past the canvas ballies, CAMERA PASSES a dog on a platform, a* CONTORTIONIST, *and finally rises above the head of a camel where in the background the stagecoach comes to a stop in front of a remote road ranch—an isolated outpost set up to accommodate travelers on the overland routes.*

A river, bordered by cottonwoods, threads through the vast landscape in the background. The road ranch itself is a crude, dug-out sod and log house with a rock chimney and prairie grass growing from the roof. A spotted goat stands on the roof, grazing.

The medicine show troupe consists of various painted wagons and tents that are set up around the area—livestock including mules, oxen, ponies, and horses tethered nearby.

On the stage the LITTLE PERSON ACROBATS *perform. There are various esoteric anatomical charts painted on the back of the stage. A skeleton stand is propped up on one side of the stage. Surrounding these charts are mysterious symbols, signs, and numbers. Burlap curtains hide the exits to stage left and right. An old upright piano is set upstage right draped with an Indian blanket. On top of the piano is a line of various-sized jars filled with alcohol and containing tapeworms, livers, kidneys, hearts, lungs, and other animal organs on display. A small band of musicians is playing an Irish fiddle tune on the stage, and this music is what we've been hearing as* PRESCOTT *approached.*

The small audience for the show is a mix of rough-looking frontier folk and more finely dressed Eastern travelers, two men and a woman, just passing through. The acrobats finish their act and cartwheel offstage.

EXTERIOR. RISE (ABOVE MEDICINE SHOW CAMP)—DAY.

FULL FIGURE ON PRESCOTT as he dismounts and moves into a CLOSEUP, looking down at the medicine show from the top of the break. He scans the faces in the audience as though looking for someone in particular.

EXTERIOR. MEDICINE SHOW CAMP/STAGE—DAY.

PRESCOTT'S POINT OF VIEW—CLOSER ON MEDICINE SHOW as an eight-year-old black boy enters the stage doing a buck and wing tap dance for the audience with a deadpan face. The minstrel band plays a rousing mountain tune. Some of them are seated in straight-backed wooden chairs and some standing behind them. They are all very straight-faced and somber, wearing tattered three-piece suits and derbies covered with prairie dust. In fact, everything is covered in dust.

The awning above the wagon stage reads: "Dr. Eamon MacCree's Kickapoo Indian Medicine Show." Other signs and banners around the stage and wagon announce: "Kickapoo Indian Sagwa—The Mystery Cure of the Plains"; "Guaranteed to Cure—Dyspepsia, Scrofula, Ghout, Worms, Liver Complaint, Catahrr, or any Disease of the Blood, Bone and Nervous System"; "Lost Manhood Cured with Buffalo Salve"; "Wizard of the Plains—Dr. Eamon MacCree."

CAMERA PANS THE AUDIENCE as two clowns improvise their way through the crowd in a slapstick style, harassing a ranch hand, and stumbling over a fat woman, and behind the band, and the audience immediately warms to them. They are both dressed in long overcoats and painted faces. The STRAIGHT MAN wears oversize work boots and a top hat. The COMIC wears a derby with large clown shoes.

As the minstrel band keeps playing, camera discovers the PETRIFIED MAN with a sign to that effect. He is laid out flat on his back on a low pallet, wearing only a white loincloth. He is ghostly white and stiff as a board, except for his ice-blue eyes which dart around in their sockets as though looking for a way to escape.

EASTERN WOMAN *and* EASTERN MEN *look on in shock at the* PETRIFIED MAN, *the men trying to shade the woman from the hot sun. The* COMIC *and* STRAIGHT MAN *interrupt by taking the umbrella and making their way to the stage. The* EASTERN MEN *are not amused. They demand the umbrella be returned and with a whack on the head the* CLOWNS *return the property.*

The CLOWNS *lift the* TAP DANCER *offstage and with a whistle stop the band. The* COMIC *raises his hand and taps a count to begin a song. But just as the* COMIC *and* STRAIGHT *prepare to sing something upbeat, the band plays a sad song. The* COMIC *and* STRAIGHT *begin to cry and* CAMERA MOVES CLOSE *to see their sobbing faces.* COMIC *wipes his tears and nose with* STRAIGHT's *hand, and when* STRAIGHT *realizes what's going on he hits* COMIC *over the head and knocks him to the stage.*

EXTERIOR. RISE (ABOVE MEDICINE SHOW CAMP)—DAY.

PRESCOTT *is crouched down, putting rope hobbles on the three spare horses while his saddle horse just stands by waiting, with his reins on the ground.* PRESCOTT *turns over his shoulder as he works with the horses' legs and looks down at the medicine show. Sounds of audience laughing in background.*

CUT TO:

EXTERIOR. MEDICINE SHOW STAGE—DAY.

The two CLOWNS *continue with another skit as the audience eats it up.*

COMIC *(looking around)*: Nice little place you got here. Kinda lonesome . . .

Laughter from audience.

COMIC *(continuing)*: . . . but it's nice just the same.

STRAIGHT: Yeah, I got me this place rent-free. Government couldn't give it away.

More laughter from audience.

COMIC: How's that?

STRAIGHT: On account of it's haunted.

COMIC: Aw, I ain't afraid a' no ghosts.

STRAIGHT: Well, that's good, 'cause they're liable to come waftin' in and outta here any old time.

COMIC: You actually, I mean, you, uh, you seen 'em here, waftin'?

STRAIGHT: Yeah, I seen 'em waftin', but you don't gotta fret yerself. All's I do is sing 'em my ghost song and they scat like a scalded dog.

COMIC: How's that song go, 'case I need it?

STRAIGHT: Goes like this here:

As STRAIGHT MAN starts to sing his ghost song, the musicians make eerie sounds on their instruments, and weird rattles and clanks are heard offstage. The COMIC is getting more spooked. The audience is right with them.

STRAIGHT *(singing)*:
Old jawbone,
The old jawbone on the almshouse wall,
The old jawbone,
The old jawbone on the almshouse wall.

The old jawbone on the almshouse wall,
It hung fifty years on that whitewashed wall.
It was grimy, and gray, and covered with gore,
Like the souls of the sinners who'd passed before.

Old jawbone,
The old jawbone on the almshouse wall,
The old jawbone,
The old jawbone on the almshouse wall.

At twelve o'clock near the hour of one,
A figure appears that will strike you dumb.
He grabs your hair by the skin of the head.
He grabs you fast until you are dead.

EXTERIOR. RISE (ABOVE MEDICINE SHOW CAMP)—DAY.

PRESCOTT *on the ridge. He remounts his saddle horse and starts to descend the hill toward the medicine show at a walk, leaving the other horses behind and hobbled.*

CLOSE ON PRESCOTT as he rides slowly down the ridge, his eyes still searching the stage and the audience for someone. The background sounds of the medicine show continue over.

CUT TO:

EXTERIOR. MEDICINE SHOW STAGE—DAY.

The STRAIGHT MAN *exits upstage, still singing, leaving the* COMIC *alone and trembling on stage. (See* STRAIGHT MAN *offstage changing quickly into ghost costume.)*

COMIC *(to* STRAIGHT *as he exits):* Hey! Where you goin'! You gotta teach me that song! I don't know that song! You gotta teach it to me. *(To the audience.)* You seen that fella? That fella here? He, uh . . . HEY!! You gotta teach me that song!!

A GHOST *(played by same actor who plays* STRAIGHT MAN*) in white rags and carrying an Indian rattle enters the stage from behind the* COMIC, *who doesn't see him. Audience reacts to the* GHOST.

The GHOST *creeps up behind the* COMIC *and shakes the rattle in his ear. The* COMIC *wheels around to face the* GHOST. *His hair stands straight up on his head. Then a chase ensues with the two of them running all over the stage and the musicians backing them up with appropriate "chase" music. The audience is cheering and laughing.*

CUT TO:

EXTERIOR. RISE—DAY.

PRESCOTT *makes his way down the rise.*

EXTERIOR. MEDICINE SHOW STAGE—DAY.

As the COMIC *is chased off by the* GHOST *who slaps him across the ass with a "slapstick" (two boards on a leather hinge that pop when they strike together), the audience roars and applauds.*

EAMON MACCREE'*s son,* REEVES, *enters the stage from behind the burlap curtains. As he speaks to the audience they begin to calm down in anticipation of the next event on the program.* REEVES *is young and energetic with wild eyes and has learned his showmanship well from his father. He wears a derby and a three-piece suit. He immediately has the attention of the audience.*

REEVES: Good folks! You've been very kind and receptive to our little presentation here today. And just on account of that, we got a special surprise in store for you all. We don't usually like to bring her forth in front of so many folks on account of her terrible shyness.

REEVES *moves down to the edge of the stage.*

REEVES: Now, if you folks don't mind bunchin' up a bit there. We need plenty of room for this act.

The audience moves back away from the stage, following REEVES's *instructions. (*COMIC *and* STRAIGHT *come down front and help push the audience back away from the stage.)*

REEVES: That's right. Just bunch up and allow some room and I guarantee you won't be disappointed. Now, get ready for some of the wildest horsebackin' yer likely to ever see this side of the Brazos! Miss Velada MacCree!! The Kiowa Warrior Princess!!!

The band strikes up a rousing tune as VELADA, EAMON's *half-breed Indian daughter, explodes from around behind the stage standing in the saddle of a paint. She falls back and her body hangs off the back of the horse in a tail drag. The paint gallops down, past the audience into the open area. When she stops and rises, her eyes meet* PRESCOTT's. *He watches her carefully from the rise near the show.*

VELADA *performs an incredible series of acrobatic feats as the paint maintains circles in front of the stage at a gallop. She swings down under the horse's neck and up the other side; she rides backward. She stands on her hands and walks the horse's back. She swings under the belly and flips herself back up.*

She is only about seventeen with long black hair swirling around her like a hurricane. Her face is not pretty but strong and powerful, taking more after the Indian side than the Irish. Her eyes have a vulnerability yet are frightened and wild like an animal trained to do tricks without knowing why.

CLOSE ON PRESCOTT, still riding toward the show at a walk. He sees VELADA *and seems to recognize her. This is the one he's been looking for. He urges his horse toward the show.*

CLOSE ON REEVES still on the stage platform. He sees PRESCOTT *approaching the back of the audience and stares hard at him.*

REEVES'S POINT OF VIEW OF PRESCOTT IN MEDIUM SHOT—OVER AUDIENCE.

CLOSE ON REEVES recognizing PRESCOTT. *He grows alarmed and rushes offstage to find his father.*

ANGLE ON VELADA through audience, still galloping in circles, doing her stunts. The crowd is cheering and throwing hats.

ANGLE ON PRESCOTT watching VELADA *carefully.*

CUT TO:

EXTERIOR. MEDICINE SHOW CAMP/BEHIND STAGE—DAY.

REEVES *running behind the wagons and livestock, CAMERA TRACKING PAST the* LITTLE PERSON ACROBATS *arguing, etc.*

EXTERIOR. MEDICINE SHOW CAMP/EAMON'S WAGON—DAY.

ANGLE ON REEVES as he runs up to one of the wagons where his father, EAMON, *is seated on the slat steps chugging on a bottle of his own Kickapoo Indian Tonic. A mixed-breed* PROSTITUTE *who works for the road ranch is sitting on* EAMON'S *knee, sharing his bottle and giggling. The band is still heard in the background, accompanying Velada's act to the whooping of the crowd.*

ANGLE ON EAMON MACCREE seated on the wagon with the PROSTITUTE *on his lap. He is permanently drunk and very Irish. He wears a top hat, but he's affected certain Indian ways, like two long braids with beaded cinches, a beaded vest under an English overcoat with tails, heavy trousers, and cavalry boots to the knee. He carries a long-barreled navy Colt revolver on his hip and holds a gnarly blackthorn walking stick to steady himself. He is enjoying his two favorite things—booze and reciting limericks—when his son interrupts him.*

EAMON *(to himself or anyone)*:
There was a young man from Siam
Who said, "I go in with a wham,
But soon lose my starch
Like the mad month of March
And the lion comes out like a lamb."

EAMON *gives the* PROSTITUTE *a pinch and she runs off, giggling.*

ANGLE ON REEVES running up to EAMON.

REEVES *(out of breath)*: Guess who's come?

EAMON: Who's come? Shem the Sham? Or the Fairy Frog, perhaps?

REEVES: That horse swapper.

EAMON: Horse swapper. What horse swapper . . . ?

REEVES: The one you swapped Awbonnie for!

EAMON: Aaah, yes! *That* Horse Swapper.

REEVES: He's come back!

EAMON *struggles to rise, but he's too drunk to catch his balance. He holds his hand out for* REEVES *to take ahold.*

EAMON: So, he's come back. Help me up outta the bog like a true son would aid an ailing father!

REEVES *grabs his hand and hoists him to his feet as* EAMON *struggles with his bottle of tonic and his walking stick. He straightens his top hat and hitches his gun belt up.*

REEVES: What's he come back for?

EAMON: How in the name a' Shamus should I know what he's come back for! You take me for a geomancer?

REEVES: What if he's come for his horses back and his loot?

EAMON: We ate his horses outside Omaha! Or do we forget the hard times so easy? They couldn't run a lick anyhow. Miserable snides.

EAMON *staggers off in the direction of the medicine show stage with* REEVES *doing his best to support him. CAMERA PANS WITH THEM as they pass and stays on their backs as they move away toward the stage.*

REEVES: Say Awbonnie ran off on him or something? She hated being traded like that. I knew we were gonna have to pay for this.

EAMON: You shoulda been born a female the way you whine and whimper. Now, git me to the bloody stage! We've got tonic to sell!! Miracles to perform! The whole Prairie is festering for our remedy!!

They weave their way toward the stage with EAMON *waving his walking stick dramatically. In the background the* LITTLE PERSON ACROBATS *chase the* PROSTITUTE, *waving money at her.*

CUT TO:

EXTERIOR. MEDICINE SHOW/AUDIENCE—DAY.

ANGLE ON PRESCOTT, through the audience, mounted on his horse at the rear of the small crowd. He stares over their heads at VELADA *as she comes to the end of her performance.*

ANGLE BACKSTAGE as REEVES *props* EAMON *up and heads for the stage. He takes* EAMON's *bottle away from him.*

PRESCOTT'S POINT OF VIEW over the audience—to see VELADA *complete a series of tricks and bring the paint to a stop. She and the paint make a bow to the audience, and as she rises with the horse she sees* PRESCOTT *and recognizes him. The band pumps up their accompaniment.*

ANGLE ON PRESCOTT. He tips his hat toward her, but his face remains grave and somber.

CLOSE ON VELADA. She seems alarmed by PRESCOTT's *presence.*

PRESCOTT'S POINT OF VIEW.

As VELADA *turns her horse away and gallops off, disappearing behind the stage and the medicine wagon, the audience applauds and cheers.*

The musicians resolve the music and break into a prolonged military snaredrum roll (prelude music for EAMON's *entrance).*

ANGLE ON STAGE as REEVES *barges through the burlap curtains with an armload of various hats—sombreros, derbies, Stet-*

sons, etc. *He encourages the audience to come in closer to the stage.*
COMIC *and* STRAIGHT *urge audience back closer to the stage.*

REEVES: Now! Good people of the Open Plains! May I have your attention, please! Please come in closer now. Before we reach our grand finale, I would like to introduce to you the man who is responsible for our little pilgrimage into your forgotten territory.

ANGLE ON EAMON backstage, behind the burlap curtains, waiting to enter. He is checking his bullets in the cylinder of his pistol and then replacing it in his holster. He pulls out another abalone-handled revolver from his belt and checks it for bullets. He pulls out a small silver flask of some kind of medicine and takes a belt, swirling it in his mouth and gargling, then spitting it out. He is continually catching his balance through all this with his walking stick. The voice of REEVES from the stage continues to play over all this.

EAMON *(to himself as he checks pistols)*: Horse swapper. Couldn't outrun their own feed bill.

ANGLE ON REEVES.

REEVES: That's right, folks. The U.S. government may have turned their Yankee backs on you, but there is one amongst us who has not forgotten your lonely plight.

ANGLE BACKSTAGE.

EAMON *(to himself)*: Lonely plight. Your "lonely plight." *(Now yelling.)* Your lonely, lonely plight!

CLOSE ON REEVES reacting to EAMON, then back to audience.

REEVES: That you yourselves have had to face. A man who was captured at a very young and tender age and taken into the hands of the dreaded Kiowa/Comanche.

ANGLE BACKSTAGE.

EAMON: Filthy heathen.

EAMON *spits his "medicine" out and adjusts his top hat.*

REEVES'S VOICE *(continued over)*: Not only did he live to relate the
tale, but he was also initiated into a deep . . .

EAMON: "A deep and mysterious secret." *(He grabs his crotch and
adjusts it.)* It's all in the palm a' me hand, me hand. It's all in
the palm a' me hand.

ANGLE ON REEVES from behind audience's heads.

REEVES: None other than my father! Doctor and Professor Emer-
itus of Herbal Prairie Medicines—The Honorable Eamon
Monachain MacCree!!!!!

*The crowd cheers. ANGLE ON CROWD, THEN PAN-
NING BACK TO THE STAGE to see EAMON come stagger-
ing on, pistol in hand, blackthorn walking stick in the other. He
manages to catch himself and present a reasonably sober demeanor.*

EAMON *(under his breath to audience)*: Ya miserable prairie vermin.

*A haunting ballad sets a mysterious tone in the audience as EAMON
pulls himself together for his big pitch.*

*EAMON moves slowly downstage and rests his hands on his walking
stick. He stares into the faces of the audience and speaks very directly
to them in a semi-hushed voice, as though he were letting them in
on the secret of their lives. He is a master orator with a voice like
a preacher. The audience is instantly mesmerized.*

EAMON *(to the audience)*: Fair people of the raging wind— Have
you ever fallen into a terrible fever? Or ever known one
who has?

*CLOSE ON FACES IN AUDIENCE as they pick up this
almost frightening shift in tone from EAMON. There is enough of the
truth in what he is saying and the way in which he presents it that
they relate it directly to their own experience.*

EAMON *(continuing over)*: Not the fever of the lovesick or forlorn or the cowardly, yearning for the hearth of a New England home, but the real burning fever. The fever of the Demon Prairie and all its attendant ills!

ANGLE ON PRESCOTT OVER AUDIENCE. He keeps his eyes on EAMON *and starts to walk his horse slowly around the back of the audience, heading for the wagons of the medicine show caravan.*

ANGLE ON EAMON as he plunges deeper into their psyche, knowing he has them in his hand.

EAMON: I was cast into the eye of just such a fever as a wee lad myself. Not more than a day's ride from the very soil on which we now stand.

EAMON'S *voice continues over as CAMERA FOLLOWS PRESCOTT.*

EAMON *(voice-over)*: Surrounded by my primitive captors! Painted faces. Bodies greased in the fat of the bearded buffalo. A language unknown to me—being a native son of Erin. A language of the Spirit World!

A heavy gust of dusty wind swells up as if what he's saying has conjured up spirits.

ANGLE ON EAMON who is now completely submerged in his own fabrication.

EAMON: I had succumbed to that state betwixt and between. A foot in two worlds, as it were. Uncertain as to whether I had, indeed, passed over and was now in some cruel dream realm of life. I was lost and adrift in a swirling phantasma! And there a vision appeared to my raw young mind! Two eyes like the eyes of a red-tailed Hawk! Teeth like a prairie Wolf! It hung above my face in a twirling specter. And then it spoke its name. This was indeed a man and not an apparition! An authentic Medicine Man from the dreaded Kiowa/

Comanche Nation. And what he was about to share with me was a sacred secret which no white man had ever been made privy to. A secret which I have brought with me here today to share with each and every one of you.

EXTERIOR. MEDICINE SHOW CAMP/BEHIND STAGE—DAY.

ANGLE ON PRESCOTT as he rides around behind the wagons, searching for VELADA.

The voice of EAMON *and the piano ballad continue over this.*

EAMON *(voice-over)*: The Ancient Sagwa Serum, stolen from the Kickapoo!

As PRESCOTT *approaches* EAMON*'s wagon,* REEVES *comes rushing out of the wagon, struggling with a big basket full of labeled tonic bottles packed in straw to sell to the audience.*

REEVES *almost runs straight into* PRESCOTT*'s horse but avoids the collision and moves around him. Their eyes meet and then* REEVES *rushes off with the basket, toward the stage, looking back over his shoulder at* PRESCOTT. PRESCOTT *continues on, searching for* VELADA.

EXTERIOR. MEDICINE SHOW CAMP/STAGE—DAY.

ANGLE ON THE STAGE as REEVES *enters with the basket of tonic bottles.* EAMON *has now changed gears and is full swing into his Salesman Pitch. Piano shifts mood.*

EAMON: It saved me from the Valley of the Shadow, ladies and gentlemen, just as it can save you! Even with our limited supply I am prepared to make an exceptional offer here today. The first bottle of our Tonic is free with a dollar purchase of the second. That's two bottles for the price of one! And we guarantee your money back if you aren't completely satisfied with the immediate results.

REEVES *moves downstage with the basket of bottles and starts pulling them out and offering them to the people who move in closer to the stage.*

The audience starts holding up dollar bills to the stage and crowding in to get their bottles. EAMON *smiles and hands a bottle out to one of the people.* REEVES *starts taking in the money and handing out bottles from the basket.* COMIC, STRAIGHT, *and* TAP DANCER *join* REEVES *and start handing out bottles and collecting money. The* LITTLE PERSON ACROBATS *collect money from the crowd.*

EAMON: Now, when I tell you that Kickapoo Sagwa is a miracle of medical knowledge, I'm not just tootin' my pipe. Say the malady is unknown to you—it hasn't got a name—it's just a feeling of malaise in the blood or the brain. You take a small tin cup full or straight from the bottle—take it straight down and reap the wonderful benefits. You'll feel a glow of health and well-being move through your blood, right down to your very core.

EAMON *backs away and slips out through the burlap curtains as* REEVES, COMIC, STRAIGHT, *and* TAP DANCER *continue to hand out bottles and collect money as the people clamor for more. The band starts up a lively tune.* STRAIGHT *walks over to the* PETRIFIED MAN *and gives him a drink of water.*

EXTERIOR. MEDICINE SHOW CAMP/BEHIND STAGE—DAY.

ANGLE ON VELADA as she appears on her paint, from behind a tent.

ANGLE ON PRESCOTT as he stands outside Eamon's wagon. He stares at VELADA *and then quietly enters the wagon.*

INTERIOR. EAMON'S WAGON—DAY.

PRESCOTT *enters and has to stoop slightly in the cramped quarters. The walls of the wagon are covered with posters of the show from various locations, photographs of the various acts, buffalo rugs,*

Indian blankets, all the paraphernalia acquired in Eamon's journeys.

PRESCOTT *peers at all the artifacts, then finds a photograph of two young Indian girls. Under each girl are their names, written in white ink: "AWBONNIE" and "VELADA."*

EXTERIOR. BACKSTAGE—DAY.

EAMON *staggers down the steps muttering and heads for his wagon.*

INTERIOR. EAMON'S WAGON—DAY.

PRESCOTT *stares hard at this photo. He is visibly moved by it. His eyes find another photo of an Indian woman. Beneath it is written "Silent Tongue." He studies them carefully, as though searching for something hidden within them.*

EAMON *suddenly barges into the wagon, still drunk and in need of another bottle.*

PRESCOTT *turns and just stands there facing him. Pause.* EAMON *stares at him a second.*

EAMON: Ah, yes! The Horse Swapper! I heard you were payin' us another call. "Prescott"? Wasn't it "Prescott" something?

PRESCOTT: You've a stout memory, sir.

EAMON: "Roe." "Prescott Roe." That's it. It's the Irish rings a bell with me. Never forget a kinsman. Not in this forsaken desert. Even those that barge right in.

PRESCOTT: Forgive me, sir.

EAMON: Not a word of it. I've grown accustomed to the primitive for some time. In fact, I prefer it by now. It's the primitive that feeds my livelihood.

He offers a bottle of tonic to PRESCOTT.

EAMON: Drink?

PRESCOTT: Thank you, no.

EAMON: Never partake of the jar. Remember that as well. A restraint I hold no envy for. Set yer bones down, then.

PRESCOTT *finds a seat on a barrel but seems stiff and awkward, painfully formal. They stare at each other a moment with* PRESCOTT *finding it difficult to speak. Pause.*

EAMON: How's the daughter, then? Did she serve yer backward son well?

Another pause, with PRESCOTT *struggling in himself.*

PRESCOTT: She's . . . . She's passed.

Pause. EAMON *stares at him with no sign of remorse but nevertheless surprised at the news.* PRESCOTT *is seized with grief but tries to control it.*

EAMON: Well— A deal's a deal, after all. She was healthy when we made the swap. Far healthier than yer son, by all accounts. Can't very well return the horses now, anyway. It's been a year or more. Poor excuse for horseflesh in the first place.

PRESCOTT: I don't want the horses. It's not yer fault she died. It happened in childbirth. And the child went with her.

EAMON: I see. Well, there's no way to account for the trauma of birth, is there, now. That's one I've never got over, myself.

Pause. PRESCOTT *unable to speak.*

EAMON: Well—what is it, then? How are we honored by your sudden visit?

PRESCOTT: It's my son. He's taken a terrible grief over her. He's fallen even deeper inside himself. Weeks now. He refuses to eat, speak. He just . . . . He just stands over her corpse like a lost soul. Just watching. Speaking tongues. Guarding. As though she were still in the world.

EAMON: Well, he'll get over that business. You know the way the heart goes. Give him time. After all, it was only his first wife.

PRESCOTT: He won't get over it. He'll perish.

EAMON: He was well on that road before he even met my daughter, if I remember your description of him correctly.

PRESCOTT: He's worse now. His mind's completely gone.

Pause as EAMON *grows more uncomfortable in* PRESCOTT's *presence.*

EAMON: I still fail to see the object of your return, Mr. Roe. Insanity's beyond my domain. I restrict myself to the physical woes.

PRESCOTT, *with great difficulty, gathers his words together.*

PRESCOTT: Your second daughter. I wish to purchase your second daughter at the same exchange. She may distract him from this endless mourning. It's the only chance I have to save my son. I've brought three sound mounts. Well broke to saddle or to pack. I have them hobbled now, at the top of the rise, yonder.

EAMON: I'm not a bottomless pit of daughters, Mr. Roe. I've only one left now, apparently.

PRESCOTT: My son will die without her. He's close to it now.

EAMON: She draws the crowds like flies now with her pony act. She's our main attraction.

PRESCOTT: I'll throw in extra.

Pause.

EAMON: What extra? We've got livestock aplenty. I don't need more horses who can't get out of their own way.

PRESCOTT: Coin.

EAMON: Ah— Cash, then? The melody rises. Must've stored some up over the years, eh? All that trade with cavalry and cattlemen. Not much use for coin out there in the flats, is there, Mr. Roe? Weighs a body down.

PRESCOTT: My son is dying of grief, sir. His mind is gone. I'll pay you anything you ask. What more can a father do?

EAMON: A desperate man should never lay all his cards on the table when doing business, Mr. Roe. Well, let's have a look at what you've brought. Then we can talk more reasonably.

PRESCOTT: I'd be obliged, sir.

They head for the wagon door and exit.

EXTERIOR. MEDICINE SHOW CAMP/EAMON'S WAGON—DAY.

REEVES *is heading toward it with the empty basket full of straw packing. In the background, the crowd is dispersing and the band is playing a rousing number.*

REEVES *stops when he sees* EAMON *and* PRESCOTT *coming out of the wagon. They descend the steps of the wagon.*

REEVES *(to* EAMON*)*: We're flat out of tonic.

EAMON *looks up to see* REEVES *and seems suddenly nervous by this encounter.*

EAMON: Good! That's good. That's the plan. Means they'll come back tomorrow, then. Tell them we'll have plenty for all, tomorrow evening.

EAMON *and* PRESCOTT *begin to move away as* REEVES *stops them and moves toward them.*

REEVES *(to* EAMON*)*: What's *he* come for?

EAMON: Ah. Just a bit of business. You carry on with the customers, now, before they all dwindle away on us.

REEVES: Where's Awbonnie?

EAMON: She's—

> EAMON *squirms and turns to* PRESCOTT, *trying to get out of it.*

EAMON: Mr. Roe, do you remember my son, Reeves, by chance?

PRESCOTT: I do.

> REEVES *moves in closer to* PRESCOTT.

REEVES: How is my sister, Mr. Roe?

> *A pause.*

PRESCOTT: She's passed.

> REEVES *is stunned. He drops the basket. His eyes search* PRESCOTT *and* EAMON.

EAMON: It was an accident, Reeves. She died in childbirth. Couldn't be helped. Now, you go attend to the business at hand.

> REEVES *is boiling with emotion between anger and grief. He moves into* PRESCOTT *and glares in his eyes.*

EAMON: He's always carried an unnatural fondness for his half sisters, Mr. Roe. You can't blame him for that.

PRESCOTT: I don't.

> REEVES *suddenly makes a lunge toward* PRESCOTT, *but* EAMON *deftly clubs him between the shoulders with his walking stick, bringing* REEVES *to the ground with a single blow.*

> PRESCOTT *makes a move to help* REEVES *to his feet, but* EAMON *stops him.* PRESCOTT *stares at* EAMON, *unable to comprehend his cruelty.*

EAMON *(to* PRESCOTT*)*: Leave him! He's got a temper like a red snake. Best to let him stew 'til it passes through him.

ANGLE ON REEVES on the ground.

REEVES *(to* PRESCOTT*):* What have you come back here for!!

PRESCOTT *just stares at him, then he looks up to see* VELADA *on her camel in the distance, behind* REEVES.

REEVES *wheels around in the dirt to see* VELADA *riding by on the camel. He then turns back to look at* PRESCOTT. *His eyes jerk toward* EAMON. *He suddenly puts things together and understands* PRESCOTT*'s intentions. His eyes are blazing with anger at his father.*

REEVES *(to* EAMON): What're we all for sale now?

CLOSE ON EAMON who decides to postpone the deal with PRESCOTT *until* REEVES *cools down. It's apparent that he's some-what afraid of* REEVES*'s temper.*

REEVES *picks himself up and goes running off toward* VELADA *in the background.* PRESCOTT *watches him go.*

EAMON: I think it best, given the circumstances, that we continue with our business another time, Mr. Roe.

PRESCOTT: It can't wait!

EAMON *(coldly):* It will *have* to wait.

CLOSE ON PRESCOTT as his eyes go toward VELADA.

PRESCOTT'S POINT OF VIEW. He sees REEVES *running up to* VELADA *and the camel and then the two of them walking away and disappearing behind the wagons in the distance, looking back toward* PRESCOTT.

CLOSE ON PRESCOTT. Background sound of the band playing.

EXTERIOR. BURIAL TREE SITE—DUSK.

CLOSE ON TALBOT with flames of bonfire reflecting off his face.

CLOSE ON TALBOT'S HANDS as they meticulously sort through small piles of bird and animal bones, rocks, and feathers, stacking them in various arrangements around the fire—some in small circles, others in miniature pyramid shapes, like ritual tokens to the corpse.

CAMERA PULLS BACK SLOWLY to see TALBOT *working on his hands and knees around the fire, collecting the small objects and building them into groups as he speaks to himself and the corpse.*

TALBOT: Still. You stay. Still. Stay.

TALBOT's *eyes raise to stare at the corpse in the burial tree.*

TALBOT'S POINT OF VIEW of corpse. The night wind blows her hair. Sound of a distant coyote. A night hawk. The crackling fire.

CLOSE ON TALBOT as he returns to his ritual arranging of bones.

TALBOT *(sorting bones)*: They watch. They have their eyes. They listen for you, but I know them. I am guarding. They can't see me. They think my mother took me. *(He laughs.)* They think that.

TALBOT *looks back at corpse.*

HIS POINT OF VIEW of corpse silently resting in the burial tree.

CLOSE ON TALBOT still watching corpse.

TALBOT: I will stay until your hair has blown away. No bone will stay. No last bone.

TALBOT'S POINT OF VIEW OF CORPSE—CAMERA MOVES IN VERY SLOWLY toward the face of the corpse, getting very tight on the closed eyes. Suddenly the eyes of the corpse snap open and her neck jerks toward TALBOT.

ANGLE ON TALBOT, terrified, scrambling to his feet and backing away.

TALBOT'S POINT OF VIEW of the GHOST OF AWBONNIE, *standing on the corpse glaring down at* TALBOT *from the tree. She is dressed in a long white gown. Her face is painted in fierce war makeup with a wide white stripe running from top to bottom across her nose. One side of her face looks like the corpse of* AWBONNIE, *and the other side is sneering and evil looking. There is an almost masculine physical strength to her presence. She moves in violent bursts of speed and then total stillness.*

ANGLE ON TALBOT as he watches her.

CLOSE ON TALBOT, eyes wild with terror, not knowing if this vision is actual or in his own mind. He backs up closer to the fire. He tries to speak but no words come.

ANGLE ON GHOST as she leaps down from the tree and pushes him to the ground. Her eyes are like knives.

GHOST: You're a dog. A low dog. Tying me here.

TALBOT: Awbonnie? Is it you?

GHOST: You must leave here! Now! Leave this place!

TALBOT: They will tear your body.

GHOST: Let them! Let them devour me so I can fly.

TALBOT: I'll die without you!

The GHOST *suddenly attacks* TALBOT, *flying at him with incredible force, knocking him flat to the ground.*

GHOST: You keep me bound here out of your selfish fear of aloneness! I am not your life!

The GHOST *leaps off him.*

ANGLE ON TALBOT. He is stupefied by this attack.

The GHOST appears standing over the corpse. She leaps to her feet and runs to the burial tree. She attacks the corpse, ripping the blankets away, tearing at it with her teeth and hands. She throws pieces of the corpse at the fire.

TALBOT: No! Nooo!!

TALBOT rushes toward the fire and tries to save the fragments of the corpse from burning.

ANGLE ON GHOST as she throws the blanket and the rest of the corpse at TALBOT's feet.

GHOST: It's *you* that must release me. Throw this body to the wind! Let them feed it to their young!

The GHOST leaps off the tree and disappears into the night.

COMPLETELY BLACK SCREEN in silence except for the faint sound of the rattling bones from the tree, then the fire and wind coming in.

ANGLE ON TALBOT as he moves slowly toward a blanket, picks it up by one corner, then goes about collecting all the pieces of the corpse and placing them on the blanket as he drags it along. A coyote in the distance. He holds the body tight to his chest and looks out to the darkness.

DISSOLVE TO:

EXTERIOR. MEDICINE SHOW CAMP—DAWN (NEXT DAY).

(Piano over.)

The light is barely breaking on the horizon. Very still except for the sounds of a lyrical piano duet and a slow shuffle tap dance. All the livestock stand with their heads down, sleeping. The camel, buffalo, mules. The overland stage is gone now, leaving the road ranch looking even more desolate in the background.

ANGLE ON PETRIFIED MAN lying on his back under a wagon, an Indian blanket draped over him. His eyes are wide open and darting as he listens to the piano and the sound of the tap dance.

ANGLE ON TAP DANCER dancing on the stage.

ANGLE ON VELADA AND THE PAINT as she leads the horse past the sleeping ACROBATS, *past the feet of the* TAP DANCER, *past the camel, and out into the open space in front of the wagon caravan and stops. She looks back toward the sound of the piano. Her eyes survey the surrounding country and the morning light.*

CAMERA MOVES IN ON CLARINET PLAYER AND PRAIRIE GIRL. They are leaning on each other dreamily as though they've spent the whole night there. Their hands overlap each other as they finger the keyboard. An empty bottle sits beside them.

ANGLE OVER THE TAP DANCER. VELADA *walks on, leading the paint toward the river behind the road ranch. The dog passes by and the CAMERA CRANES UP to see the river.*

REVERSE ANGLE ON PIANO DUET and the TAP DANCER *continuing.*

EXTERIOR. MEDICINE SHOW CAMP/RIVER— DAWN.

ANGLE ON VELADA as she walks into the river and stops. VELADA *grabs the mane of the paint and swings up into the saddle. She rides the horse at a walk right up the middle of the river.*

CLOSE ON VELADA as she looks around, seeming to sense something in the air. She listens. A meadowlark in the distance. The leaves of the cottonwoods rattle in the breeze. Everything is peaceful with the distant sounds of the piano and the tap dancer gliding over.

She pulls the paint up and stops again, listening closely to the air. The sound of a grackle. The piano now barely audible in the distance.

VELADA *turns her horse in a full circle in the river, scanning the surrounding area for something. She walks the horse on up the river. She stops the horse again.*

CLOSE ON VELADA *as she turns the paint in the river again, looking intensely at the banks but seeing nothing. The sound of the paint splashing in the water.*

She stops still, listening. Complete stillness, then the snakelike hissing sound of a rawhide riata lariat whipping through the air.

VELADA'*s eyes—wide with fear.*

The leather rope slashes down across her face and snares her around the waist, also encircling the paint's neck. The paint rears out of the water, but VELADA *hangs on to her mane and neck as the rope is jerked tight around the two of them, lashing* VELADA'*s arms to her sides.*

CLOSE ON PRESCOTT'S HAND *dallying the rope on his saddle horn and taking up all the slack. His hand with the rope and the saddle horn are all that's seen.*

CLOSE ON VELADA *on the paint trying desperately to free herself from the rope. A dark canvas feed sack is suddenly brought down over her head. The* SCREEN GOES BLACK *for a second.*

CLOSE ON PRESCOTT'S HANDS *jerking into frame and lashing a rawhide latigo around the sack to keep it shut tight.* VELADA *thrashes to free herself, but she's caught like a rabbit in a snare.*

WIDE ANGLE IN THE RIVER. PRESCOTT *on his saddle horse is dragging* VELADA *and the paint across the river by the rope.*

The saddle horse lunging powerfully as he pulls the paint splashing along behind him.

CUT TO:

EXTERIOR. MEDICINE SHOW CAMP—MORNING.

CLOSE ON THE CAMEL raising his head toward the distant sounds of the struggle upstream. Sound of the piano duet over.

ANGLE ON ROAD RANCH as PRESCOTT *leads* VELADA *to the rise.*

ANGLE ON THE PETRIFIED MAN, his eyes darting to where the noise is coming from.

EXTERIOR. MEDICINE SHOW CAMP/STAGE—MORNING.

ANGLE ON TAP DANCER looking toward the rise as the horse heads up.

CUT BACK TO:

EXTERIOR. RISE (ABOVE MEDICINE SHOW CAMP)—MORNING.

WIDE ANGLE ON PRESCOTT dragging VELADA *and the paint up the side of the rise (from the opening shot), where Prescott's other horses are tethered.*

CLOSER ON PRESCOTT, pulling up alongside his three spare horses and dismounting.

PRESCOTT *goes quickly to* VELADA, *who is still struggling on the paint. He is holding some latigo straps in his teeth, which he takes out and starts strapping* VELADA'S *legs to her saddle fenders with. He tries to calm her and be as gentle as he can without scaring her further. He talks quietly and firmly to her. As soon as she hears his voice she begins to calm down.*

PRESCOTT (*as he ties her to her saddle*): I am sorry about this. I truly am. There was just no other way to get it done. I'll not harm you. I swear on an oath to that.

CLOSE ON VELADA with the canvas bag covering her head. She stops struggling now and becomes very still. Her head pivots slowly, searching for his voice, like a blind person.

PRESCOTT *gathers up his other horses once he's finished securing* VELADA *to the paint's saddle. He mounts his saddle horse with all the other horses in tow plus the paint and* VELADA. *He looks back over his shoulder at her before he spurs his horse.*

WIDE ANGLE—PRESCOTT *closes his legs on the saddle horse and they all pull out at a lope with* VELADA *hanging on. They gallop away from CAMERA into the vastness of the flat prairie.*

CAMERA PANS AWAY AND BACK to the sleeping medicine show camp, seen in LONG SHOT from the top of the rise. The piano duet over, in the distance.

EXTERIOR. MEDICINE SHOW CAMP—MORNING.

The stray dog is seen again as he trots toward Eamon's wagon, jumping over the PETRIFIED MAN.

ANGLE ON COMIC AND STRAIGHT as they play cards under tent.

EXTERIOR. MEDICINE SHOW CAMP/NEAR EAMON'S WAGON—MORNING.

CLOSER ON THE DOG as he trots toward Eamon's wagon with his nose to the ground.

CAMERA ARRIVES ON EAMON'S WAGON as the stray dog trots on, out of frame.

INTERIOR. EAMON'S WAGON—MORNING.

CAMERA MOVES IN ON EAMON asleep on the floor in a drunken stupor with one leg straddling the PROSTITUTE. *He is sprawled out under an old Indian blanket, snoring loudly and groaning. He tosses from side to side and starts grabbing his crotch, as though in the midst of an erotic dream. The* PROSTITUTE *rolls away from him and slips out quietly through the door, taking a bottle of* EAMON'S *"medicine" with her.*

CAMERA MOVES IN TIGHT *on* EAMON'S *sweating face as he tosses.*

CUT TO:

EXTERIOR. WIDE-OPEN PRAIRIE/STAKED PLAINS (1850S)—DAY.

EAMON'S DREAM IN BLACK AND WHITE.

The sun-bleached bones and carcasses of slaughtered buffalo are strewn out across the land as far as the eye can see.

In the very midst of the sea of bones is the lone figure of a YOUNG INDIAN WOMAN. *She is stooped over and slowly leading a pony pulling a travois. Buffalo bones are stacked high on the pony's back and on the travois. The woman keeps stooping over and picking up bones and stacking them on the travois as the pony slowly walks along, its head hung low.*

CLOSER ON THE INDIAN WOMAN. *She is recognized as the same woman from the photograph in Eamon's wagon—"Silent Tongue." She looks up from her work and suddenly freezes, seeing something approaching in the distance.*

CLOSER ON BUFFALO HUNTERS *and the* BOY.

They move toward CAMERA and then stop and stare at SILENT TONGUE. *One of the hunters is recognized as young* EAMON MACCREE. *The young boy is* REEVES. *They appear to be more animal than human with clothing made of pelts and hides, ammunition belts strapped across their chests, knives in beaded Indian scabbards dangling from their waists. They all carry Sharps buffalo guns, even young* REEVES. *The pack animals behind them are loaded high with buffalo hides.*

CLOSE ON SILENT TONGUE, a panic creeping into her eyes as she studies them across the distance.

ANGLE ON HUNTERS and the BOY watching her.

HUNTER: That's the one. Had her tongue cut out for lyin' to her headman.

EAMON: How can you tell from this far off?

HUNTER: She's the only Bone Picker out here. Got to be her. Go on! Try yer Irish Luck. She won't make a sound. I'll guarantee that.

EAMON turns to the young REEVES.

EAMON *(to the BOY)*: Turn yerself around! Or the banshees'll get ya!

The boy stares up at his father. EAMON grabs him by the shoulders and turns him so that he's facing away from SILENT TONGUE.

EAMON *(to the BOY)*: Do it now! If I catch ya lookin' I'll thrash ya 'til yer knees buckle!

The BOY stays still with his back turned to them. EAMON drops his gun and takes off his ammunition belts. The other HUNTER chuckles and prods him.

HUNTER: Might as well let him see how it's done.

HUNTER'S POINT OF VIEW over the face of the young REEVES, onto the backs of the men to see SILENT TONGUE in background as she sees EAMON's intentions and takes off running through the sea of bones. The pony takes off in fear, the travois flying off its back.

HUNTER: Quick, now! She's got a jump on ya!

THE BOY'S FACE IN FOREGROUND as EAMON takes off, running away from CAMERA, chasing SILENT TONGUE. CAMERA stays on the BOY's face.

Laughter of the HUNTER *over the* BOY's *face.*

CLOSE ON SILENT TONGUE—TRACKING FAST
with her as she stumbles through the bones, fleeing EAMON. *She*
looks back over her shoulder and runs on.

CLOSE ON EAMON—TRACKING FAST, as he crashes
after her in hot pursuit.

CLOSE ON THEIR FEET, running and stumbling through
the buffalo bones.

ANGLE ON SILENT TONGUE as she turns an ankle and
falls into the bones. She scrambles on her hands and knees, desper-
ately trying to escape EAMON's *attack. Her mouth opens wide as*
though trying to scream, but no sound comes out. Her mouth is pitch
black and painted around her lips with black.

ANGLE ON EAMON as he swoops down on her like a hawk.

ANGLE ON HUNTER as he grabs the boy REEVES *by the*
shoulders and turns him around to witness his father's actions. The
HUNTER *hoots at him.*

HUNTER: Look here, boy! This is what you got up ahead, son.

The BOY *has his hands over his eyes. The* HUNTER *pries the* BOY's
hands away.

CLOSE ON THE BOY witnessing EAMON *as he rapes* SILENT
TONGUE.

BOY'S POINT OF VIEW. At a distance, EAMON *is seen*
rolling the Indian woman over in the bones and mounting her
savagely.

VERY CLOSE ON SILENT TONGUE as her black mouth
opens in a silent scream.

CUT TO:

INTERIOR. EAMON'S WAGON—MORNING.

RETURN TO COLOR.

ANGLE ON EAMON.

EAMON: I made her my legitimate wife!! Don't forget that! Don't ever forget that!

EAMON is jerked out of his nightmare by REEVES, up to a sitting position.

CLOSE ON EAMON, his eyes wide, still half in the dream, as he stares at his son's face.

CLOSE ON REEVES in a rage. He shakes EAMON by the shoulders.

REEVES: So you went and swapped her after all! Just like Awbonnie!!

EAMON is sweating and panicked. He speaks to REEVES as though referring to his nightmare.

EAMON shoves REEVES away from him, then starts to come to his senses. He searches around frantically for a bottle to cure his hangover, the bottle that the prostitute took with her. REEVES is beside himself with rage.

REEVES: You'll go straight to Hell for this! You might as well have killed them both with your own hands!

EAMON uncovers a half-empty bottle of tonic and knocks it back, taking a long pull. This seems to bring him into the present.

EAMON: Killing? Now he's on about killing! It's too early in the morning for killing. The sun's barely cracked.

REEVES: When did they leave?

EAMON: Who leave? Stop talkin' in riddles.

REEVES: Velada and Roe! They're gone! When did they take off?

EAMON stares at him, baffled.

REEVES: As though you didn't know?

EAMON: Gone?

> EAMON *staggers to his feet and starts thrashing around in a rage, searching for his pistol, boots, and clothes.*

EAMON: I suppose he pilfered that paint, too! Goddamn his Irish hide!! Get my mule tacked out! Be quick!!

> REEVES *exits the wagon as* EAMON *straps his pistol on.*

EAMON: That paint was worth a hundred dollars!

> *CLOSE ON REEVES, angered by his father's words.*

> *CUT TO:*

> *EXTERIOR. OPEN PRAIRIE—SAME MORNING.*

> *WIDE SHOT OF PRESCOTT at a killing jog with all his horses plus* VELADA *and the paint.* VELADA *still has the feed sack covering her head. They trot along through barren country for a while, then* PRESCOTT *pulls up and dismounts.*

> *CLOSER ANGLE ON PRESCOTT as he walks back to* VELADA *and stands beside her horse.*

PRESCOTT: Bend forward so's I can unlash that nose bag.

> *CLOSE ON VELADA, who refuses his order.*

PRESCOTT: Do as I say!

> VELADA *does what she's told and* PRESCOTT *unties the feed sack. He speaks to her as he goes about this business.*

PRESCOTT: I don't expect you to think kindly toward me for my actions. But I'm asking you to listen to me with your heart.

> PRESCOTT *pulls the feed sack off her head.*

> *CLOSE ON VELADA gasping for breath, her eyes wide as she looks into* PRESCOTT's *face, then takes in her surroundings. She is*

scared but self-contained. She stares hard at PRESCOTT, *not knowing what to expect from him. She listens to him intently, trying to comprehend his motives. She remains silent.*

PRESCOTT: Do you remember me? The self-same man who purchased your sister? Your brother must have told you.

VELADA *just stares at him, making no acknowledgment.*

PRESCOTT: You must remember. She was joined in wedlock to my son. I chose between you at the time.

VELADA *still makes no sign of recognition toward him. She just stares into his face like a frightened animal.*

PRESCOTT: There's no way to foresee the outcome of a thing. What I had hoped to be my son's salvation became his ruin. Your sister . . .

PRESCOTT *begins to break down but tries to control it.* VELADA *watches him closely as he struggles with his emotions.*

PRESCOTT: Your sister was his light. He thrived in her company. She . . . . Your sister . . . . She has since . . . died.

CLOSE ON VELADA taking this news slowly. Her face contorts in grief, then she throws her head back. She suddenly throws herself forward on the paint's neck, making an unearthly animal scream.

The paint leaps out into an open gallop, knocking PRESCOTT *to the ground with* VELADA *hanging on to the mane, her legs still strapped to the saddle.*

ANGLE ON ALL THE OTHER HORSES who panic at VELADA's *scream and bolt along with the paint. They all go galloping off following* VELADA *and the paint into the open prairie.*

Gold coins fly out of the saddlebags.

ANGLE ON PRESCOTT desperately caught on foot. He struggles to stand and chases after his saddle horse but soon slows down to a walk when he realizes the futility of catching up.

PRESCOTT'S POINT OF VIEW of VELADA *and all the horses at a gallop, diminishing in the distance.* PRESCOTT *begins picking up some of the spilled coins and collecting them, then straightens up and stares off into the distance after* VELADA.

ANGLE ON PRESCOTT left alone on foot in the vast landscape. Off his horse he seems much more vulnerable and pathetically alone as he gazes around at the land, realizing his plight and that of his son.

CLOSE ON PRESCOTT.

DISSOLVE TO:

EXTERIOR. BURIAL TREE SITE—DAY.

CAMERA FINDS TALBOT sitting in the tree gently stroking the long black hair of the corpse.

CAMERA MOVES IN CLOSE ON HIS FACE with an aura of madness. His eyes stare down at the corpse as though searching for a sign from Awbonnie.

TALBOT: If you could give me a sign. Some sign so I'd know how to find you. Take me with you, Awbonnie.

ANGLE ON A DEER, seemingly hearing TALBOT. *The deer takes off into the long grass.*

DISSOLVE TO:

EXTERIOR. OPEN PRAIRIE—AFTERNOON.

*(Voice-over—*EAMON *singing.)*

HIGH WIDE ANGLE OF EAMON on his mule and REEVES *on horseback, at a walk with a packhorse in tow. SLOWLY THE CAMERA CRANES DOWN. They are on the trail of* VELADA *and* PRESCOTT. EAMON, *with his top hat and roaring drunk, is singing an Irish ballad at the top of his lungs to the landscape at large.*

EAMON *(singing)*:
>The divil he came to the man at the plough
>Saying, "One of yer family I must take now."
>
>Said he, "My good man, I've come for your wife,
>For I hear she's the plague and torment of your life."
>
>So the divil he hoisted her up on his back,
>With a rightful, tightful, titty filet,
>The divil he hoisted her up on his back,
>And landed at Hell's hall-door with a crack.

>REEVES, *grim and determined, stares at the ground as they go, searching for signs of Prescott's horses. He is smoldering with animosity toward his father.*

REEVES: Aw, break it off, will ya! Now's not the time for brayin'! Yer daughter's been absconded with, in case you've forgot!

EAMON: Aah, the daughter, the daughter! That's right! Had to be some good reason we find ourselves adrift in the lone prairieeee!

>EAMON *takes another belt from his bottle of tonic and continues his ballad in full force as* REEVES *keeps hunting the ground for sign.*

EAMON *(singing)*:
>There were two other divils looked over the wall,
>They said, "Take her away or she'll murder us all."
>
>"Now, I've been a divil the most of me life.
>But I ne'er was in Hell 'til I met with yer wife."
>
>So it's true that the women are worse than the men,
>For they went down to Hell and were threw out again.

>EAMON *takes another long belt, as they continue on horseback.*

REEVES: You've got a lot of salt calling yerself a father at all.

EAMON: It was forced upon me by cruel nature! Never had a say in the business. No, sir, a father is not my calling in this life. This is true. "Wizard of the Plains!" is more to my liking.

EAMON *makes a grand gesture to the horizon line and takes another drink.*

EAMON: "WIZARD OF THE PLAINS!"

REEVES: Shoulda shot his hide the second he rode into camp.

EAMON: Who? Roe? He seemed a reasonable man to me.

REEVES *turns back to* EAMON *in his saddle.*

REEVES: Reasonable? How do you find yerself siding with him and not with yer own daughters?

EAMON: He's an Irishman! And a gentleman, I believe. Horse-thievery's his main transgression and, believe me, he'll pay through the teeth for that! That paint was worth more than both daughters and you thrown in to boot!

REEVES *turns to the front again.*

REEVES: It shames me to be the son of a pig.

EAMON: You'll grow out of it. Just thank yer stars you weren't born a half-breed like yer demon sisters.

They ride on, AWAY FROM CAMERA. EAMON *takes another belt and recites another of his favorite limericks.*

EAMON:
There was a young lady from Ulster
Whose friends they thought they had lost her
'Til they found in the grass
The marks of her ass
And the knees of the man who had crossed her.

DISSOLVE TO:

EXTERIOR. MEDICINE SHOW CAMP/STAGE—SAME DAY.

ANGLE ON THE COMIC AND STRAIGHT MAN in the midst of another skit. They seem on edge and keep eyeing the audience warily as they say their lines. Hostile voices of the road ranch owners and their partners are heard over this. The audience is much smaller this time and much rougher.

COMIC: What time you say the three o'clock train go out?

STRAIGHT: Three o'clock train? Why, that train go out exactly sixty minutes past two o'clock.

COMIC: Tha's funny.

STRAIGHT: Why's that funny?

COMIC: Fella at the depot tol' me it went out exactly sixty minutes before four o'clock.

STRAIGHT: Well, you won' miss yer train nohow.

Potatoes are thrown at the actors, accompanied by hostile voices. The COMIC *and* STRAIGHT *try to duck the potatoes and continue with the skit.*

RANCH HAND # 1: That serum couldn't cure a well man!

ANOTHER VOICE: This is a business here! We don't need no carnival trash!

More potatoes sail past the actors as they try to continue.

COMIC *(to* STRAIGHT*)*: Excuse me, uh. Which is the other side of the street?

STRAIGHT: Other side of the street? Why, the other side of the street is just across the way.

COMIC: That's funny. I asked the fella across the street and he said it was over here.

More potatoes and hostile voices.

STRAIGHT: Well, ya can't depend on everything you hear.

The audience charges the stage and leaps up on the platform after the actors. COMIC *and* STRAIGHT *run for their lives followed by the musicians, all jumping off the stage and running down the road with the audience chasing them, throwing potatoes. The* TAP DANCER *and* LITTLE PERSON ACROBATS *are running as well. A* BUFFALO HUNTER *trips, and* COMIC *and* STRAIGHT *run back, kicking him.*

ANGLE ON THE KIOWA BRAVE as he just stands there, continuing to beat a steady rhythm on his drum.

ANGLE ON THE ROAD RANCH. The PROSTITUTE *stands alone, holding a parasol.*

DISSOLVE TO:

EXTERIOR. PRAIRIE—LATE AFTERNOON.

Sound of PRESCOTT'*s jingle-bobs on his spurs.*

CLOSE ON RATTLESNAKE.

CLOSE ON PRESCOTT'S WEATHERBEATEN BOOTS AND MEXICAN SPURS trudging along through the dust.

CAMERA PULLS BACK TO FULL FIGURE ON PRESCOTT WHILE STILL TRACKING WITH HIM. He is exhausted and hungry, but he keeps going. He sees something in the distance and comes to a stop.

PRESCOTT'S POINT OF VIEW. At a distance he sees VELADA *astride her paint, just standing in the open and facing him. She has all of Prescott's horses in tow with their halter ropes in her hand. She has managed to free herself from the latigo bindings.*

CLOSE ON PRESCOTT. He is baffled by this appearance.

PRESCOTT'S POINT OF VIEW (LONG). VELADA *keeps staring at him, then suddenly turns her mare along with the other horses and moves away from* PRESCOTT, *disappearing behind a rise.*

ANGLE ON PRESCOTT as he runs into frame and away from camera off toward the spot where he saw VELADA.

CUT TO:

EXTERIOR. PRAIRIE—DAY.

(Music over.)

WIDE SHOT OF THE MEDICINE SHOW TROUPE strung out in a long line, caravaning across the immense space.

CLOSER ON THE COMIC AND STRAIGHT, drinking and playing cards on a flatbed wagon.

STRAIGHT: We're headin' east now, aren't we?

COMIC: East? East? This is east?

STRAIGHT: I'm sure we're headin' east. Your deal.

They pass a LONE MAN on foot, heading in the opposite direction. He carries a huge pack on his back and is pushing a small wooden wheelbarrow filled to overflowing with supplies and covered with a sheet of canvas. Cooking pots and frying pans hanging from the wheelbarrow make a hollow knocking sound. The COMIC yells out to him as he passes.

COMIC *(to LONE MAN)*: Where to!

LONE MAN: Land!!

STRAIGHT: You can have it!

The COMIC and STRAIGHT laugh to each other and pass the bottle. STRAIGHT raises the bottle toward the LONE MAN and yells out to him.

STRAIGHT: Hey! We've lost our leader!!

The LONE MAN continues on without stopping or turning back, heading determinedly toward oblivion. The troupe continues.

EXTERIOR. BURIAL TREE SITE—NIGHT.

*CAMERA PANS OFF FIRE TO CLOSE ON THE
GHOST.* TALBOT *is seen sitting across from her with the glow
from the bonfire illuminating his face. He clutches the shotgun.*

GHOST: You turn your back on me? You think you can
refuse me?

TALBOT: I remember you.

GHOST: I was sold like a slave! And now you want to keep me
a slave in death! I died giving birth to your child! A child I
never wanted!

TALBOT *breaks down. He begins to weep openly.*

TALBOT: I hold—on to you.

GHOST: Did you think I would love you for that?

TALBOT: Take me with you.

GHOST: You have no right to ask me that! You belong in this
world, not mine. You owe me my freedom!

TALBOT *slowly raises his head to look at her.*

TALBOT: How?

GHOST: Let my body burn. Throw it in the fire!

TALBOT *slowly shakes his head, refusing her. He holds the shotgun
tightly.*

GHOST: Then take your own life! Do it. It's in your hands. Place
that gun in your mouth and set me free.

TALBOT *stares at her. The fire crackles and sparks.*

GHOST: I warn you now— If you don't do this thing I ask, then
a curse will fall on your father's head.

The GHOST *begins to sing a haunting Indian melody. She stops
suddenly.*

GHOST: Yes. Do it. Your suffering is nothing compared to what your father will have to bear.

TALBOT *weakens. He places the barrel in his mouth.*

GHOST: Do it. Do it! Do it!!

He pulls the shotgun out of his mouth and points it at the GHOST, *emptying both barrels. She has vanished. He runs to the burial tree.*

EXTERIOR. PLAINS—SAME NIGHT.

CLOSE ON PRESCOTT in blue moonlight. His eyes are covered with the gold coins. There are more coins lined up on his forehead, chin, and neck. His face is deathly still.

CAMERA MOVES TO DISCOVER VELADA in the distance, in full moonlight, sitting on her pony with Prescott's other horses around her. She is staring at PRESCOTT *from a distance. She walks her horse in closer to* PRESCOTT, *leading the other horses along with her.*

CLOSE ON PRESCOTT'S FACE covered with the coins. He doesn't breathe. The hooves of the paint and other horses come into frame by PRESCOTT's *head, but still he remains motionless.*

ANGLE ON VELADA dismounting and walking up to PRES-COTT. *He just lies there like a dead man. She bends down and reaches out for the gold coins.*

Suddenly PRESCOTT's *hand leaps out and grabs* VELADA *by the wrist, twisting her off balance. Coins fly, horses bolt. They roll down the sand dune. Before she can put up a fight,* PRESCOTT *is on top of her, pinning her arms to the ground. He speaks to her in an urgent whisper.*

PRESCOTT: I was wrong to steal you against your will, but you must help me. I have no one else. You must help me now.

CLOSE ON VELADA. She struggles, but PRESCOTT *keeps her pinned down. She is staring, terrified, into* PRESCOTT's *desperate face. He releases her and sits back. She moves away from him on her back.*

PRESCOTT: If your sister hadn't come, he'd have never made it. Do you understand me?

VELADA *stares hard at him.*

PRESCOTT: You must replace her. It's his only chance.

VELADA: I am not my sister!

PRESCOTT: I can make you the same offer I made your father. You'll be richer than him by far. Gold coin. Three mounts. The very ones you tried to steal.

VELADA *stares into his eyes.*

PRESCOTT: Three horses. Gold. I am begging you now. You'll be free of your father.

ANGLE ON VELADA. She relaxes but keeps staring at PRES-COTT, then turns and looks back at all his horses.

VELADA: Four horses. *And* gold.

ANGLE ON PRESCOTT realizing she has agreed, and he nods his head to seal the bargain.

CUT TO:

EXTERIOR. PLAINS—SAME NIGHT.

REEVES *is off his horse, on foot, staring hard at the maze of hoofprints left by Prescott's horses when they ran off with VELADA. He is totally confused by the tracks.*

ANGLE ON EAMON astride his mule with the packhorse behind him. EAMON tilts back the last drop from the very last bottle of tonic and tosses the bottle out into the prairie with a crash of glass.

EAMON: That's it! That's the last of it. Time we turned back, now. It's dark thirty.

REEVES *(staring at tracks)*: They've gone into a whirlwind here. I can't make this out.

EAMON: It's time we turned back, now! The banshees'll get us.

REEVES: We're not turnin' back! There's sign here. We just got to figure it out.

EAMON: Yer not gonna track a plainsman out into flatland he knows better than the inside of his own mouth! We've probably passed him a dozen times already and never even known it. Now, mount up and point these leatherheads for home camp. We've wasted enough time on this malarkey.

REEVES: Are you tellin' me you want to just leave her lost? Abandon her?

EAMON: I've got an entire troupe back there loaded with tonic. They're ready to move out! They'll pack out without me and steal me blind. I'm not tradin' off me livelihood to pursue a rat-tail horse thief!

REEVES: What about Velada!

EAMON *(turning his mule)*: She'll make do. She's a Kiowa.

REEVES: She's your daughter!

EAMON: She's a Kiowa first!

> EAMON *heads away from* REEVES *with his mule and packhorse.* REEVES *remains afoot.*

REEVES: You'll never make yer way back without me! You've lost yer sense of the prairie! If you ever had one to begin with. *(Pause.)* "Wizard of the Plains!"

> EAMON *stops his mule, realizing the truth of what* REEVES *says. He turns back to* REEVES.

EAMON: Are you refusing me, then? Yer own father?

CLOSE ON REEVES.

REEVES: Yer no father to me.

EAMON draws his huge dragoon pistol and approaches REEVES on the mule. REEVES just stands there, facing him on foot.

EAMON: Mount that miserable geldin' now before I separate your ears.

REEVES holds his ground and just stares back at him.

REEVES: You haven't got the sand.

Pause as EAMON reconsiders and slowly reholsters his gun. His hands are shaking. His tone becomes more pleading now.

EAMON: Try, if you will, son, to put yerself in my boots. I've grown accustomed to an hourly lubrication over the years, and I can't just sever the connection like that. It's not like a woman. I've got to get back to my supply a' tonic!

REEVES turns away from him coldly and heads for his horse. EAMON is becoming more desperate.

EAMON: Think of the troupe, then! You remember what happened to us in Wichita when they almost lynched the whole lot of us. We can't just leave them back there in limbo.

REEVES mounts his horse and stares back at EAMON.

EAMON: There's no percentage in this cruelty! None whatsoever! You got to think of yer poor father in this. It's me, now! I'm the one that's suffering, not her! She's an Indian. They were born to suffer!

REEVES: Follow.

REEVES wheels his horse around and heads off away from EAMON, following the tracks he's decided on. EAMON tries to catch up on his mule, towing the packhorse behind.

EAMON: Heathen children! The lot.

CUT TO:

EXTERIOR. PRAIRIE—NIGHT.

CLOSE ON A WOLF TRACKING FAST as it runs through long buffalo grass.

ANGLE ON THE GHOST running furiously across the prairie with both arms stretched high above her streaming hair. In each hand she holds a medicine knife with deer-hoof handles and leather thongs lashing in the night wind. An eerie blue light is cast across the GHOST's face.

She swoops down suddenly on the running wolf and plunges both knives deep into its back. The wolf buckles into the dirt with the GHOST on its back.

CUT TO:

EXTERIOR. PRAIRIE—PRESCOTT/VELADA CAMP—NIGHT.

CLOSE ON KNIVES shooting into PRESCOTT's back.

VELADA is awakened and sees PRESCOTT rolling in pain. Her face recoils in terror as she sees the two deer-handled knives plunged into PRESCOTT's back.

VELADA rushes toward PRESCOTT and pulls out both knives, then hurls them into the night.

CLOSE ON KNIVES hurtling through black space then suddenly vanishing.

CLOSE ON VELADA. She whirls around toward PRESCOTT who has rolled onto his back, gasping for air.

VELADA: My sister is sending you her thoughts!

PRESCOTT: It was just a pain. *(Pause.)* Your sister is dead.

VELADA: She is my mother's weapon! She is moving on you now with vengeance.

PRESCOTT *struggles to stand.*

PRESCOTT: We must get to my son! We got to get to him fast.

VELADA: I cannot move against my sister.

PRESCOTT: Your sister is dead!! She's gone!

CLOSE ON PRESCOTT contorted in the light of the campfire.

VELADA: She is more alive than you.

PRESCOTT: We've made a bargain.

CLOSE ON VELADA.

DISSOLVE TO:

EXTERIOR. PRAIRIE—MEDICINE SHOW WAGON—SAME NIGHT.

WIDE ANGLE OF MEDICINE SHOW caravaning through the night, a haunting melody over this.

LITTLE PERSON ACROBAT *(singing)*:
   If I was home I'd lay in my bed
   Prop up my feet and pillow my head
   Gaze out the window and look at the sky

ANGLE ON ONE OF THE LITTLE PERSON ACROBATS playing a squeezebox and singing to the PETRI-FIED MAN *as the wagon bumps along.*

LITTLE PERSON ACROBAT *(singing)*:
   And rest while the bluebirds
   Go whistling by
   Go whistling by.

PETRIFIED MAN'S POINT OF VIEW of full moon racing.

DISSOLVE TO:

EXTERIOR. BURIAL TREE—MORNING.

CLOSE ON STOCK OF SHOTGUN chopping into the dirt at TALBOT's *feet.*

ANGLE ON TALBOT digging a circle in the earth surrounding the burial tree with his shotgun. He works desperately, as though it were a matter of life and death. The circle represents some kind of barrier in his mind to protect the corpse, which is still hanging tattered in the tree. He stops suddenly and looks out across the huge space in the distance.

TALBOT'S POINT OF VIEW.

EXTREME LONG SHOT OF THE DISTANT FIGURES OF PRESCOTT AND VELADA approaching on horseback. They are unrecognizable over the distance.

BACK TO SCENE.

TALBOT *drops his shotgun and quickly climbs the tree so that he arrives right next to the corpse bundle. He stops there and looks out at the approaching figures.*

OVER TALBOT'S SHOULDER, with the black hair of the corpse blowing through frame, we see PRESCOTT *and* VELADA *getting closer with all the horses, still unrecognizable to* TALBOT.

ANGLE ON TALBOT, who starts working frantically to untie the corpse bundle from the scaffold. He speaks out loud to her as he works.

TALBOT: Haycha. She won't steal you. She won't take you from me. She brought a demon with her. No. No!!

CUT TO:

EXTERIOR. PRESCOTT'S CAMP/NEAR BURIAL TREE—MORNING.

MEDIUM LOW ANGLE ON PRESCOTT AND VELADA as they approach with their horses. PRESCOTT *pulls up.* VELADA *and the other horses stop behind him.*

CLOSER ON PRESCOTT staring off in the distance at the smoke from TALBOT's *fire. He speaks to* VELADA.

PRESCOTT: You must go to him by yourself. Say nothing to him about me.

PRESCOTT *stares at her.*

PRESCOTT: All he needs is a voice. A kindness. I expect nothing from you but to comfort my son. All you must do is to show him some affection.

VELADA *looks up but seems reluctant and uncertain.*

PRESCOTT: Go now! Save him!

VELADA *takes off toward* TALBOT*'s fire.* PRESCOTT *stays behind with the other horses.*

VELADA *turns and looks back at* PRESCOTT *as her horse continues toward the smoke.*

ANGLE ON PRESCOTT, who raises his hand softly to her, bidding good luck.

ANGLE ON VELADA as she turns back toward CAMERA while PRESCOTT *rides out of frame in the background with the other horses, leaving* VELADA *and the paint alone in the open space.*

EXTERIOR. BURIAL TREE SITE—MORNING.

REVERSE ANGLE BEHIND VELADA and the pony as they approach the bonfire and the burial tree.

CLOSE ON VELADA as she rides. The sounds of rattling bones and the crackling of the bonfire. Smoke drifts across her face.

VELADA'S POINT OF VIEW (from horseback height). She sees the empty burial tree with the bones and tin cans blowing gently in the wind. The corpse is gone. No sign of TALBOT. *The place is deserted.*

VELADA'S POINT OF VIEW of the bonfire as she rides past it at a walk.

MEDIUM CLOSE ON VELADA AND PAINT as she stops and gazes around the area.

VELADA'S POINT OF VIEW (from horseback, panning left to right). She sees the burial tree and the bonfire. There is a haunted, lonely sense of the place. (Music throughout this.)

ANGLE ON SIDEWINDER SNAKE scurrying through the sand.

Suddenly, from a short distance away, TALBOT *is seen running away from her like a frightened animal, clutching the corpse to his chest and carrying the shotgun. CAMERA SWINGS FAST WITH HIM, THEN CONTINUES RAPIDLY PANNING AND WINDS UP ON THE PAINT'S HEAD.*

CLOSE ON PAINT'S HEAD, nostrils flaring, ears pricked.

CAMERA MOVES INTO CLOSEUP OF VELADA'S FRIGHTENED FACE.

VELADA *urges her pony in* TALBOT'*s direction but not chasing him. She is as frightened by his appearance as he is by hers.*

CLOSE ON TALBOT as he suddenly jumps out in front of VELADA. *There is a complete madness in his eyes now as he clutches the corpse tightly and holds the shotgun on* VELADA.

ANGLE ON THE PAINT AND VELADA as the pony whirls around and VELADA *reins him in so that she's facing* TALBOT.

CLOSE ON TALBOT, terror in his eyes. He relates to VELADA *as though she were the* GHOST.

TALBOT: You can do what you want with my father, but this body is mine! It belongs to me!

ANGLE ON VELADA, then back to TALBOT.

TALBOT: You will never separate us! I hold this body.

ANGLE ON VELADA as she slowly dismounts and takes a step toward him.

TALBOT *raises the shotgun, threatening her. She stops.* TALBOT *moves back from her, clutching the corpse to his chest.*

TALBOT: I will send you to your death a second time if you touch her.

CLOSE ON TALBOT. He studies her face.

CLOSE ON VELADA.

VELADA's *face changes to the face of the* GHOST, *then back to* VELADA's *own.*

VELADA: I am not my sister.

EXTERIOR. PRESCOTT'S CAMP/NEAR BURIAL TREE—MORNING.

ANGLE ON PRESCOTT.

EXTERIOR. PRAIRIE—DAY.

EAMON *and* REEVES, *on horseback, following Prescott's trail.*

REEVES: He's afoot now! Look at this! He's got to be afoot.

EAMON: You've not got the mental gifts to track this man. He's schemin' ya. Can't ya tell that by now? If he's afoot, there's a reason for it. He's leading us to our doom!

REEVES: Velada's escaped him. Look! Look for yourself. He's afoot. I've got him now.

EAMON: Yer an idiot! *He's* got *you!* Yer playin' right into his hand.

REEVES: She's slipped away from him, I tell ya . . .

EAMON *(to himself)*: Insanity is a sorry thing. Dear Lord in Heaven, save me from it. A Professor deserves a better fate than this. I am a European, not a savage!

EAMON *looks up at the horizon and his face goes white with fear. He keeps his mule moving forward, behind* REEVES, *who keeps studying the ground for tracks.*

ANGLE FROM THE RIDGE—CAMERA MOVES PAST small band of Kiowa warriors on a scouting party. They just stand there motionless on their ponies, watching EAMON *and* REEVES.

CLOSE ON EAMON. He lowers his eyes slowly and carefully away from the Indians and lowers his head, trying to pretend he hasn't seen them. He speaks to REEVES *in a shaky, hushed voice. His hands are trembling. His mouth goes dry.*

EAMON *(hushed)*: Whatever in the world you do now, son, don't raise yer eyes to the horizon.

ANGLE ON REEVES, who abruptly does the opposite, jerking his head toward the horizon and seeing the Kiowa.

REEVES'S POINT OF VIEW of the Kiowa, still motionless, watching them.

ANGLE ON EAMON, who tightens his voice.

EAMON: Put yer eyes back down, you fool! Don't look at 'em! Keep yer horse movin' at the same pace. Don't change stride an inch!

REEVES *turns his head back and lowers his eyes, just as* EAMON *instructs. They continue on like this, pretending they haven't noticed the Kiowas' presence. They speak to each other with their eyes lowered.*

REEVES: It's just a hunting party.

EAMON: Just a hunting party! And what do ya suppose they might be hunting? I'm tellin' ya now, if we don't turn back, their dogs will be eatin' our testicles by nightfall! Now, listen to reason! This has gone far enough!

REEVES: We're not quittin' this!

EAMON: Yer stubbornness is gonna get us skinned!

REEVES: Is it stubborn to reclaim what's ours? She was stolen from us!

EAMON: If it means our hides, then let him have her!

REEVES *jerks his head back toward his father in rage.*

REEVES: What is she to you, except a reminder of your sins!

CLOSE ON EAMON. *He is struck to the bone by this.*

ANGLE ON REEVES *staring back at* EAMON.

REEVES: We're gonna find her. Even if we both die doin' it.

REEVES *turns his gaze toward the horizon again. The Kiowa have vanished.*

REEVES: They've gone.

EAMON *looks toward the horizon slowly.*

EAMON'S POINT OF VIEW *of the empty horizon line.*

CLOSE ON EAMON.

EAMON: They'll be back. And there won't be just a handful next time. There'll be so many you'll think the prairie sprouted them. I wasn't descended from proud Irish chieftains in order to have my hide stripped away by heathens!

WIDE ANGLE OF THE TWO OF THEM *continuing their search.*

CUT TO:

EXTERIOR. BURIAL TREE SITE—AFTERNOON.

LONG SHOT—THROUGH A TELESCOPE. *We see* VELADA *crouched down on her haunches by the bonfire, roasting a snake in the fire and eating it. She keeps sticking the snake into the fire, then pulling it back out and eating it.*

EXTERIOR. PRAIRIE/NEAR BURIAL TREE— AFTERNOON.

LOW ANGLE ON PRESCOTT *lying on his belly in the long prairie grass, peering through a telescope. He is a good distance away from* VELADA *and* TALBOT, *so they can't see him. His horses are not around.*

EXTERIOR. BURIAL TREE SITE—AFTERNOON.

PRESCOTT'S POINT OF VIEW—THROUGH A TEL-ESCOPE—on VELADA *again, who continues eating, then she stops and looks toward* TALBOT, *who is unseen for the time being. She throws a piece of the snake in his direction. The telescope pans to pick up* TALBOT. *He is sitting near the fire, still clutching the corpse in his lap and the shotgun. He stares at* VELADA, *then at the piece of snake in front of him.*

EXTERIOR. PRAIRIE/NEAR BURIAL TREE—AFTERNOON.

ANGLE ON PRESCOTT looking through the telescope. He speaks softly to Talbot as he keeps looking through the telescope. (These are his thoughts to his son, spoken out loud to himself.)

PRESCOTT *(softly)*: Eat. You must eat. Take it.

EXTERIOR. BURIAL TREE SITE—AFTERNOON.

CLOSER TWO-SHOT OF TALBOT AND VELADA (not through the telescope). She continues eating and staring at him. She throws him another piece of the snake. TALBOT *watches her, then looks at the food. He is starving but reluctant to take it. She urges him to eat by nodding her head.*

Slowly TALBOT *sets down the shotgun and reaches out for a piece of the snake.* VELADA *watches him closely and keeps eating.* TALBOT *picks up the food.* VELADA *keeps urging him gently.* TALBOT *takes a bite, then begins to eat very tentatively.* VELADA *tosses him some more.*

EXTERIOR. PRAIRIE/NEAR BURIAL TREE—AFTERNOON.

ANGLE ON PRESCOTT lying on his belly in the long grass, peering through the telescope. He speaks softly to TALBOT.

PRESCOTT: Yes. Eat now. Get your strength back. That's it.

EXTERIOR. BURIAL TREE SITE—AFTERNOON.

ANGLE ON TALBOT tearing into the flesh of the snake, eating like a starved animal. VELADA *keeps tossing him more pieces, which he snaps up and devours.*

TWO-SHOT VELADA AND TALBOT. She smiles at him and moves a little closer, but he suddenly panics, drops the food, and snatches up his shotgun, backing away from her. TALBOT *clutches the corpse and eyes her suspiciously.* VELADA *offers him more food, but* TALBOT *remains wary.*

EXTERIOR. PRAIRIE/NEAR BURIAL TREE— AFTERNOON.

ANGLE ON PRESCOTT in grass, looking through the tele- scope.

PRESCOTT: Trust her. Just let her help you.

EXTERIOR. BURIAL TREE SITE—AFTERNOON.

ANGLE ON TALBOT AND VELADA. She keeps eating and offering out the food to him, but TALBOT *refuses. CAMERA MOVES INTO CLOSEUP OF TALBOT as the voice of* PRESCOTT *speaks softly, over.*

PRESCOTT (*voice-over*): Talbot. Listen to me now. You must forget about this death. Let go of it. It's poisoned you enough. Look in her eyes. She will bring you back.

SUDDEN CUT TO:

EXTERIOR. PRAIRIE—AFTERNOON.

ANGLE ON HAWK.

ANGLE ON GHOST OF AWBONNIE. She releases a huge red-tailed hawk from her hand. The wings explode across the frame, lashing past the GHOST's *face.*

CUT TO:

EXTERIOR.   PRAIRIE/NEAR   BURIAL   TREE—
AFTERNOON.

CLOSE ON THE HAWK as it swoops down on PRESCOTT,
still lying in the long grass, and attacks his head, digging its talons
into his neck. PRESCOTT *rolls over, thrashing and tearing the hawk*
away from his face.

CUT TO:

EXTERIOR. PRAIRIE—AFTERNOON.

The GHOST *raises her arms over her head.*

CUT TO:

EXTERIOR. BURIAL TREE SITE—AFTERNOON.

VELADA *stands suddenly, by the bonfire, seeing the hawk in the*
distance.

Suddenly the hawk swoops down on VELADA, *knocking her to the*
ground, then flying off.

TALBOT *runs off in a panic, taking the corpse and his shotgun.*

LOW ANGLE FROM VELADA'S POINT OF VIEW on
the ground. She sees the GHOST *of her sister run into the campsite*
and leap into the burial tree, facing her, tossing her hair like a
demon.

LOW ANGLE ON VELADA, on the ground, her terrified eyes
watching the GHOST.

CLOSE ON GHOST, in tree.

GHOST: Sister. You betray our mother! You trade yourself for
horses and gold. You are lower than the father who sold us!

The GHOST *leaps down from the burial tree and goes to* VELADA.
She crouches down next to VELADA's *head.* VELADA *tries to escape,*

but the GHOST *grabs her by the hair, then pries her mouth open and pulls her tongue out and holds on to it.*

The GHOST *draws a knife while she holds* VELADA's *tongue with the other hand. She plunges the knife into the ground next to* VELADA's *head.*

GHOST: You like bargaining with Whites, then you bargain with me, your sister. You move in close to this squirming dog. You pretend that you love him, you push your skin on his, and then take my body and you burn it. You owe this to our mother. If you run, I will hunt you down and cut your tongue out so you will never ever, never, never, never forget who gave you birth. Do you?

The GHOST *takes off, leaving* VELADA *in the dirt.*

CLOSE ON TALBOT hiding in the long grass, protecting the corpse. The wind blows the prairie grass. A distant hawk shrieks. TALBOT *looks up. A figure flies by him.*

ANGLE ON THE GHOST on horseback, galloping past through the long grass.

CUT TO:

EXTERIOR. PRAIRIE—LATE AFTERNOON, APPROACHING DUSK.

EAMON's *voice is heard singing over the following:*

CLOSE ON MULE'S HEAD as he trudges along. CAMERA PANS along the reins to EAMON's *shaking hands, then continues to discover* EAMON *in the saddle as he finishes the verse of the song. It is apparent that he's falling apart.*

EAMON *(singing):*
"My darling maid," the youth then said,
"The day is drawing near
When Irishmen will return again from all their long career.
Our holy land by God's command, the fairest land of all,

And heaven will see old Ireland free,
Bright Star of Donegal."

EAMON *yells out to* REEVES, *who is quite a ways ahead of him on
his horse, continuing on the trail of* PRESCOTT. REEVES *ignores
his father's ranting, which enrages* EAMON *further.*

EAMON: I had envisaged a better ending! One with far less pain!
Not glory or riches—just painless and numb!

Pause as they continue on their mounts. EAMON *smacks his lips
from lack of liquor.*

EAMON: It was youthful lust, out and out! Full of all its raw and
mindless pleasure! Something you, no doubt, have never
experienced. Such a faithful, honorable brother as you!

REEVES *continues on, ignoring him.*

EAMON: I could've let her wander through the bones forever!
Never touched her at all. At least I made her my legitimate
wife! Showed her some pity, which is more than I can say
for her now. Now she's paying me back, you see. Do you
understand that! She's sending her Dog Soldiers out to get
me! I guarantee you that!

*CLOSE ON EAMON as he looks all around at the horizon and
the incredible aloneness of his world. His face is full of fatigue and
terror at the prospect of Indians.*

CLOSE ON EAMON.

EAMON: Isn't that just like a Kiowa! They cut her tongue out and
she rushes back to their fold, first chance she gets! I fed her
and clothed her all those years and she deserts me, back to
her tormentors!

EAMON *suddenly senses something behind him and wheels around
in the saddle to see a much larger band of Kiowa at the same distance
as before. Maybe two dozen of them have appeared out of nowhere.
Just sitting on their ponies, staring at him over the distance.*

EAMON *draws his pistol in a panic and yells to* REEVES, *who doubles his horse around to face him.*

EAMON: Shoot yer mount and bury yerself! They've come!

EAMON *shoots his packhorse in the head. The horse rears back over itself and falls dead.*

EAMON *leaps off his saddle mule, and as he dismounts, the mule bolts and runs off.*

ANGLE ON REEVES, bewildered, caught in the confusion, whirling on his horse.

EAMON *drops to the ground, behind his dead packhorse, using him for cover. He lays his big pistol across the horse's ribs, aiming it toward the distant Kiowa.*

REEVES *stays mounted and rides over to where his father is entrenched behind the horse.*

EAMON: Dismount and shoot him! Now! They'll be on us any second!

POINT OF VIEW OF KIOWA, still just standing there watching them in eerie stillness.

REEVES: They're not moving.

EAMON *suddenly points his pistol at* REEVES*'s gelding and pulls the hammer back.*

REEVES *charges* EAMON *and kicks him solidly, sending the pistol flying.* EAMON *crumples into his dead packhorse.*

REEVES *looks back toward the horizon, standing over* EAMON *with his carbine.*

REEVES'S POINT OF VIEW. The Kiowa turn their line of ponies and file silently away, disappearing over the horizon line until they've all gone.

ANGLE ON REEVES as he turns back to his father, staring down at him on the ground.

REEVES: Looks like you'll be the one afoot now.

HIGH ANGLE ON EAMON on the ground with his dead packhorse.

EAMON: I never wanted to swap her, ya know. It wasn't my idea, it was Roe's. Besides, we needed horses at the time . . .

REEVES *turns his horse and rides away from* EAMON *at a walk, without looking back.*

ANGLE ON EAMON, struggling to his feet.

EAMON: At least leave me your carbine! I'll be worthless against them without it!

EAMON *waves his pistol in the air, but* REEVES *doesn't stop.*

EAMON: It's not just me they want, you know! They'll come for you in the night! Don't think they won't! You're not absolved from this! High and mighty! Faithful brother! They'll separate you forever from your manhood!

EAMON *staggers in circles, gazing out into the huge landscape as the sun begins to set.*

VERY TIGHT ON EAMON, staring into his own aloneness.

EAMON (*to himself*): You're not absolved.

ANGLE ON GHOST running flat out toward EAMON.

CLOSE ON EAMON seeing GHOST.

DISSOLVE TO:

EXTERIOR. BURIAL TREE SITE—LATE AFTERNOON.

The empty burial tree with the bones, tin cans, and bells making their music in the soft wind.

ANGLE ON THE PAINT, standing, tied to the tree, her mane blowing.

CAMERA PANS OFF THE PAINT, THROUGH THE CRACKLING BONFIRE, AND COMES TO REST ON TALBOT sitting asleep near the fire with his head slumped forward. His arms are collapsed at his sides in complete exhaustion. The corpse bundle lies in his lap with its black hair blowing. Smoke from the fire passes through the frame across the face of the corpse.

ANGLE ON VELADA sitting nearby and watching the corpse bundle intensely. She inches closer to the sleeping TALBOT, being careful not to wake him. TALBOT stirs, and VELADA freezes then moves in closer again, trying to reach the corpse without waking TALBOT. Sounds of the crackling bonfire and the primitive chimes from the burial tree are heard over.

CLOSER ON VELADA as she inches in toward the corpse. Her eyes are wide and frightened. She is breathing hard but trying to remain silent.

CLOSE ON VELADA'S HAND reaching out slowly toward the corpse.

Suddenly TALBOT wakes up, grabs the corpse, and rolls away from VELADA. TALBOT snatches up his shotgun and levels it on VELADA, then fires wildly, missing her by inches.

VELADA scrambles to the other side of the bonfire, facing TALBOT, who clutches the corpse tightly.

ANGLE ON THE PAINT whirling around in response to the shotgun blast.

EXTERIOR. PRESCOTT'S CAMP/NEAR BURIAL TREE—LATE AFTERNOON.

ANGLE ON PRESCOTT among his horses in the tall grass, hearing the distant sound of the shotgun. He runs toward the sound, then stops and stares out at the bonfire smoke.

EXTERIOR. BURIAL TREE SITE—LATE AFTERNOON.

TALBOT *throws* VELADA *to the ground.*

TALBOT: Who sent you here! Who sent you!

VELADA: It was your father.

TALBOT: My father?

EXCHANGE CLOSEUP BETWEEN VELADA AND TALBOT.

ANGLE ON PRESCOTT.

CUT TO:

EXTERIOR. BURIAL TREE—SUNSET.

The branches of the burial tree blow gently as the sun sets.

EXTERIOR. PRAIRIE—SUNSET.

The medicine show caravans across the prairie.

EXTERIOR. PRAIRIE—NIGHT.

TRACKING WITH EAMON running wildly with both hands clasped to his face. He stops and drops his hands from his face, staring terrified into the surrounding blackness. He calls out into the night.

EAMON: Reeves!! You can't abandon me to this!! We're flesh and blood! Reeves!!! Europeans! Don't forget that! Kings and queens! Knights of honor! Masters of an empire! Masters, Reeves! Not dogs! We can't succumb to this barbarism! We have to cling together, cling together at all costs! REEVES!

EXTERIOR. PRAIRIE—SAME NIGHT.

(Voice-over EAMON calling out to him.)

REEVES *is on his horse, still trying to follow* PRESCOTT's *tracks but losing them in the darkness. He goes in circles, staring at the ground, then doubles back and stops his horse. He hears an animal sound or a bird that could be a Kiowa call. He's completely lost now and beginning to realize his dilemma. He hears his father's voice calling out to him from a distance.*

EAMON'S VOICE *(in the dark)*: Reeves!!!!!!!

CLOSE ON REEVES on horseback. He stares into the night in the direction of EAMON's *voice, listening intensely. Another bird call pierces the still air.* REEVES *speaks quietly to his father, but more to himself.*

REEVES: Madness is a sorry thing.

CUT TO:

EXTERIOR. BURIAL TREE—NIGHT.

TALBOT, *holding the shotgun, tries to stay awake by the fire, protecting the corpse.* VELADA *watches him closely.*

EXTERIOR. PRESCOTT'S CAMP/NEAR BURIAL TREE—NIGHT.

CLOSE ON PRESCOTT among his horses, picketed at a distance from the burial tree site. He is quietly moving through the group of horses, trying to keep them quiet. He is on foot. He gives them each some grain from his hand. He strokes their flanks and necks and speaks softly to them as he goes to each one. He keeps looking off into the distance where the bonfire gleams in the night.

PRESCOTT'S POINT OF VIEW—the bonfire in the distance, the figures of VELADA *and* TALBOT *silhouetted against the flames of the bonfire.*

ANGLE ON PRESCOTT, CLOSE, THEN TRACKING CLOSE IN HIS POINT OF VIEW PAST ALL THE HORSES' HEADS as he speaks to them softly.

PRESCOTT: There, now. Soo . . . . Be still. Be still, now.

AS CAMERA KEEPS TRACKING, SHOOTING THROUGH THE HORSES' NECKS, suddenly the GHOST *appears, face-to-face with* PRESCOTT *from behind one of the horses. He is filled with terror as he confronts the painted face of the* GHOST. *She grins at him.*

GHOST: Still in the market for a wife, Mr. Roe?

She advances on him slowly, in the same way she did with Talbot. PRESCOTT *backs up through the horses. CAMERA TRACKS WITH THEM, SHOOTING THROUGH THE HORSES.*

GHOST: No— Don't go. Don't go now. You've come so far.

PRESCOTT: It's you! It's you who torments him! Why can't you set him free? He holds no blame in this. It was me who brought it on his head.

GHOST: And it's you who'll pay!

She reaches out suddenly and grabs him, pushing him to the ground with incredible strength. PRESCOTT *makes no struggle. She holds him tightly to her chest and speaks right in his face.*

GHOST: You'll never save your son. You know that, don't you? You've always known that. He's far out of your reach. Far beyond! He's in another world! You think my sister can reach him? My sister! What is she to him? Another squaw! Another Kiowa dog, sold for horses!!!

She leaps off him and suddenly appears by his horses.

GHOST: What was the price, Mr. Roe? *(Pause.)* What was the price you paid for me? *(Pause.)* Three horses, wasn't it?

She laughs at him, then suddenly runs toward the picketed horses and leaps on Prescott's saddle horse, gathering up the reins.

ANGLE ON PRESCOTT, on the ground, as he rolls toward her, trying to find his strength.

PRESCOTT'S POINT OF VIEW (low angle).

ANGLE ON GHOST, on horseback, with the other horses milling around nervously behind the rope picket. She draws a medicine knife and speaks to PRESCOTT.

GHOST *(wielding knife)*: And you think my sister's worth four? Why is she worth four, Mr. Roe? She's the same as me! She's just going to die on you. Just like I did!

She slashes the rope picket line with the knife and screams at the loose horses.

ANGLE ON PRESCOTT as he struggles to his feet.

ANGLE ON THE HORSES, bolting from the picket line and galloping off toward the bonfire in the distance.

ANGLE ON GHOST, astride Prescott's saddle horse, galloping behind the other three and spooking them.

ANGLE ON PRESCOTT as he charges on foot straight toward the GHOST *on the galloping horse.*

PRESCOTT *grabs on to the neck of the galloping saddle horse and hangs on. He is dragged along as the* GHOST *slashes at his arms with the knife. They ride off into the night, straight toward the bonfire with* PRESCOTT *being dragged and the* GHOST *trying to cut him loose.*

CUT TO:

EXTERIOR. PRAIRIE/NEAR BURIAL TREE— NIGHT.

ANGLE ON GHOST AND PRESCOTT as they battle each other on the saddle horse. The knife coming down into PRESCOTT's *shoulder, but he hangs on and grabs at her arms, trying to throw her from the horse.*

CLOSE ON THE HORSES' HEADS, nostrils flaring, in full gallop, heading for the fire.

EXTERIOR. BURIAL TREE SITE—NIGHT.

ANGLE ON VELADA'S PAINT tied to the burial tree, rearing, panicked by the oncoming horses.

CLOSE ON TALBOT, by the bonfire, staring out into the night, with the sounds of galloping horses over.

TALBOT'S POINT OF VIEW (in slow motion). He sees the horses emerging out of the blackness, galloping straight toward him and the fire.

ANGLE ON THE STAMPEDING HORSES.

VELADA *leaps into the tree and* TALBOT *dives to the ground as the horses encounter the bonfire and bolt around it. One horse charges right into the fire and out the other side, his tail and mane on fire as he gallops off into the night.*

ANGLE ON PRESCOTT being dragged at full gallop right up to the bonfire with the GHOST *slashing at his arms.*

ANGLE ON TALBOT as the horse with PRESCOTT *and the* GHOST *heads right toward him.*

ANGLE ON THE HORSE knocking TALBOT *to the ground.* PRESCOTT *loses his grip and falls in front of the fire.*

CLOSE ON TALBOT, on the ground, seeing his father.

CLOSE ON GHOST, on horseback, as she wheels the horse around and pulls up, staring down at TALBOT.

GHOST *(to* TALBOT*)*: Your father has come to save you!

CLOSE ON PRESCOTT, rolling over on the ground and looking toward TALBOT.

CLOSE ON TALBOT.

CLOSE ON VELADA as she stares at her sister.

CLOSE ON GHOST, on horseback, as she stares down at VELADA.

GHOST: Sister! You think you can replace me? You think you can replace me in his heart? Ask him. Ask him who holds his heart. He will tell you.

The GHOST *charges straight at* TALBOT *on the horse. She leans way out of the saddle and grabs at the corpse, but* TALBOT *clutches it desperately to his chest and pulls it back from her.*

The GHOST *wheels the saddle horse around again, facing* TALBOT.

ANGLE ON TALBOT as he turns on his knees to face her, still clutching the corpse to his chest.

ANGLE ON GHOST, on horseback.

GHOST *(to* TALBOT*)*: Tell her! Tell her how you can't live without me!

ANGLE ON TALBOT, on the ground, clutching corpse.

TALBOT *(to* GHOST*)*: I am holding you! You can't steal it from me! It is mine!

The GHOST *gallops down on* TALBOT, *reaching out and grabbing the corpse by the hair. She knocks* TALBOT *to the ground and rides off with the corpse.*

PRESCOTT *gathers all his strength and runs straight at her as she passes. He grabs ahold of the corpse and pulls it from the* GHOST*'s grip as she gallops on. He falls to the ground. He looks at* TALBOT *and then at the corpse.*

PRESCOTT *gets up and runs to the fire.* TALBOT *screams, running toward him.*

TALBOT: Nooo!!!!!!!!!

He looks toward his son. PRESCOTT *lets out a pained yell and throws the corpse into the raging bonfire.*

ANGLE ON THE BURNING CORPSE.

ANGLE ON PRESCOTT as he turns from TALBOT *and sees his saddle horse.*

PRESCOTT'S POINT OF VIEW. The saddle horse stands, breathing hard, steam rising off his neck and flanks. The GHOST *has disappeared.*

PRESCOTT *turns back to* TALBOT.

PRESCOTT: It's done now. It's finished. It's finished.

ANGLE ON VELADA as she turns from them and stares into the fire.

VELADA'S POINT OF VIEW. As the bonfire engulfs the corpse, slowly the painted face of the GHOST OF AWBONNIE *emerges from the flames, smiling at* VELADA.

CUT TO:

EXTERIOR. PRAIRIE/OUTSKIRTS OF SMALL RIVER TOWN—EARLY MORNING.

A bell rings in a church bell tower.

ANGLE ON EAMON'S WAGON—CAMERA CRANES UP to reveal a small river town in the background.

The CONTORTIONIST *leads the camel to reveal the* STRAIGHT MAN *and the* KIOWA BRAVE *leading a horse drawing the wagon with the* PETRIFIED MAN.

STRAIGHT MAN *(to* KIOWA BRAVE, *who remains silent as they both walk)*: You'd say we were safe now, wouldn't you? I mean if you weren't an Irish lunatic—which you're not—you'd say we were safely out of Indian country, would you? *(*KIOWA *doesn't answer.)* He had no business taking us that far out to begin with. Endangering our lives for a short con. But this looks good and safe to me. Wouldn't you say so? I mean if you were white and halfway sane?

ANGLE ON THE LITTLE PERSON ACROBATS practicing onstage.

ANGLE ON THE OXEN.

ANGLE ON THE MEDICINE SHOW BAND hoisting the PETRIFIED MAN *off the wagon. They begin to sing.*

BAND *(singing)*:
When I was a little boy,
   or so me mammy told me,
Way haul away,
   we'll haul away, Joe.

If I didn't kiss the girl,
   me lips would grow all moldy,
Way haul away,
   we'll haul away, Joe.

Way haul away,
We'll haul for better weather,
Way haul away,
   we'll haul away, Joe.

When I went away to sea,
   I didn't know no better,
Way haul away,
   we'll haul away, Joe.

ANGLE ON PETRIFIED MAN. Behind him the canvas ballies are hoisted. (Singing over this.)

PETRIFIED MAN'S POINT OF VIEW of clouds racing.

ANGLE ON THE COMIC, shaving and practicing EAMON's *pitch to an imaginary audience. He speaks with a heavy Irish accent.*

COMIC: Fair people of the raging wind. Have you ever fallen into a terrible fever? Fever. Or known anyone who has? Not the fever of the lovesick, or the cowardly, or the forlorn yearning for the hearth of a New England home.

A small gathering of children from the river town stand nearby listening intently to his speech.

COMIC: But the real burning fever. The fever of the burning prairie and all its attendant ills.

CUT TO:

EXTERIOR. PLAINS—MORNING.

CAMERA TRACKING CLOSE THROUGH THE LEGS AND HOOVES OF KIOWA WAR PONIES. The horses' legs are painted with war symbols. Animal pelts and scalps hang down in the frame, but nothing is seen of the mounted Kiowa except their buffalo-greased legs and moccasined feet.

Seen through the walking horses are the legs and feet of EAMON *trudging along. CAMERA WIDENS AND KEEPS TRACKING TO SEE EAMON, full figure, surrounded by Kiowa braves on all sides. Still, nothing is seen of the Indians except from the waist down.*

EAMON *is forced to keep walking by their continuous prodding of him with lances, clubs, and coup sticks. They yip at him as though he were a dog. They knock his silk top hat off his head, and when he tries to stop to pick it up, they stick him with lances until he's forced to move on.*

CLOSE ON EAMON'S TOP HAT as it hits the dirt and is immediately pierced with a war lance. CAMERA FOLLOWS as the lance lifts the top hat high into the air and marches along to the rhythm of the horses.

CLOSE ON EAMON. He is bruised and beaten but keeps doggedly marching on. He is in a complete delirium as he speaks.

EAMON: Remarkable, isn't it?? How things come true. I had invented this little fable. This very one I'm now living. Conjured it out of my own imagination. It was my sales pitch. Infallible. It worked every time. It was my very livelihood.

He's poked in the back of the head with a coup stick. Another lance jabs at his back. He keeps stumbling along. He breaks into a maniacal laugh. EAMON *repeats the lines from his medicine show pitch, breaking in and out of an hysterical laughter.*

EAMON: ". . . Surrounded by my primitive captors. Painted faces. A language unknown to me—being a native son of Erin."

He's cracked in the back of the head again but keeps walking on. He's on the verge of complete emotional collapse.

EAMON: I don't suppose you'd know my former wife, by any chance? Ran off on me several summers back. She was unmistakable.

A lance rips at his shoulder as he continues.

EAMON: Yes! Unmistakable! You'd know her by sight. She had no tongue, you see.

EAMON *grabs his tongue and pulls it out of his mouth, wagging it to them to demonstrate his meaning.*

EAMON: No tongue to speak of.

The Kiowa spit at him and hoot. More lances and sticks come into frame and attack him like serpents. He presses on.

EAMON: In any case—if you happen to come across her—

He stumbles and begins to break down, crying. This only stimulates the torture from the Kiowa. EAMON *struggles to hold himself together.*

EAMON: Please— Please impress upon her that I have now more than paid for her defilement. I am now completely absolved! Will you tell her that for me?

CUT TO:

EXTERIOR. PRAIRIE RIDGE—SAME TIME.

FULL FIGURE ON A LONE KIOWA WOMAN astride a black pony, set against the horizon and looking out toward CAMERA. She is wrapped in a buffalo robe.

CLOSE ON THE WOMAN, who is SILENT TONGUE. *Her lips are painted black and her dark eyes burn out into the distance.*

SILENT TONGUE'S POINT OF VIEW (over her shoulder). In the distance we see the band of Kiowa surrounding EAMON, *moving slowly away from CAMERA.*

FULL FIGURE ON SILENT TONGUE (low angle) as she turns her pony away from CAMERA and disappears over the ridge. CAMERA PANS TO KIOWA AND EAMON.

CUT TO:

EXTERIOR. NEAR RIVER TOWN/MEDICINE SHOW STAGE—DAY.

CLOSE TWO-SHOT ON COMIC AND STRAIGHT in the midst of their skit, near the river town in more civilized country.

COMIC: Nice little place you got here. Kinda lonesome but nice just the same.

REACTIONS ON AUDIENCE, more refined and well dressed than the opening audience, obviously town dwellers. They are all enjoying the show.

BACK TO STAGE.

STRAIGHT: Yeah, I got me this place rent-free. Government couldn't give it away.

Laughter from the audience.

ANGLE ON COMIC AND STRAIGHT.

COMIC: How's that?

STRAIGHT: On account of it's haunted.

COMIC: Aw, I ain't afraid a' no ghosts.

STRAIGHT *(voice-over)*: Well, that's good, 'cause they're liable to waft in and outta here any old time.

CAMERA PANS OFF THE COMIC, across the chart of the skeleton woman, and continues panning to the offstage area . . .

CAMERA MOVES THROUGH THE BURLAP CURTAINS to find one of the LITTLE PEOPLE ACROBATS, *who now plays the ghost, waiting in the wings with his white face and costume of rags, petting the stray dog and holding a bottle of booze. The* GHOST ACTOR *takes a long drink from the bottle backstage as we hear the dialogue continuing over.*

COMIC *(voice-over)*: You mean—you actually seen 'em waftin'?

STRAIGHT *(voice-over)*: Yeah, I seen 'em waftin', but you don't gotta fret yerself. All's I do is sing 'em my ghost song and they scat like a scalded dog.

COMIC *(voice-over)*: How's that song go, 'case I need it?

STRAIGHT *(voice-over)*: Goes like this here:

(Fiddle theme music begins here.)

STRAIGHT *(voice-over)*:
The old jawbone,
Old jawbone on the almshouse wall,
The old jawbone,
Old jawbone on the almshouse wall.
The old jawbone on the almshouse wall,
It hung fifty years on that whitewashed wall.
It was grimy, and gray, and covered with gore,
Like the souls of the sinners who'd passed before.

CAMERA FOLLOWS THE STRAY DOG as he leaves the GHOST ACTOR *and trots outside the open door of the medicine show wagon and down the steps.*

ANGLE ON THE STRAY DOG with his nose to the ground, trotting along through the caravan of wagons and livestock. Camera goes with him and follows him to Eamon's wagon as the song continues over.

The stray dog keeps sniffing the ground, then sniffs the stairs that lead up to Eamon's wagon. The dog hops up the stairs and enters the wagon, sniffing the whole time, as though on the trail of something. CAMERA FOLLOWS HIM INTO EAMON'S WAGON AND THEN MOVES OFF THE DOG AND ONTO THE WALLS WHERE IT FINALLY COMES TO REST ON THE PHOTOGRAPH OF SILENT TONGUE AND HER TWO GIRLS. *(The music continues over this.)*

CAMERA MOVES IN TIGHTER ON PHOTOGRAPH, CLOSE ON SILENT TONGUE. *(Singing continues.)*

STRAIGHT *(voice-over)*:
Old jawbone,
Old jawbone on the almshouse wall,
The oldjaw bone,
Old jawbone on the almshouse wall.

At twelve o'clock near the hour of one,
A figure appears that will strike you dumb.
He grabs your hair by the skin of the head.
He grabs you fast until you are dead.

Old jawbone,
Old jawbone on the almshouse wall,
The old jawbone,
Old jawbone on the almshouse wall.

DISSOLVE TO:

EXTERIOR. PRAIRIE—DAY.

The LONE MAN *on foot with his huge backpack is pushing the wheelbarrow loaded with supplies across the endless prairie.*

The LONE MAN *passes* PRESCOTT *and* TALBOT *walking. They are both exhausted.* TALBOT *has his hand on* PRESCOTT's *shoulder.*

As they pass, the CAMERA STAYS WITH THE LONE MAN AND KEEPS TRACKING WITH HIM *until he stops and turns back to* PRESCOTT *and* TALBOT, *who keep right on walking away from him without turning back. The* LONE MAN *calls out to them, but they keep right on going.*

CLOSE ON LONE MAN.

LONE MAN: Where to!

ANGLE ON PRESCOTT AND TALBOT as they just keep walking away from CAMERA without looking back.

(End credits over.)

Printed in the United States
by Baker & Taylor Publisher Services